J.L. Cowen's
Postwar Lionel Trains

O-Gauge
Reference Manual II

Motorized Units, Rolling Stock & Accessories

Robert A. Hannon
CrowsNest Publishing - Clarksville, Maryland

Lionel is a registered trademark of Lionel Trains, LLC, Mt Clements, MI.

Copyright © 2003 Patrick M. Hannon

Robert A. Hannon
11513 Crows Nest Rd.
Clarksville, MD 21029
(410)531-3244 / (410)531-3110
E-Mail: support@trainrefs.com
Website: http://www.trainrefs.com

All rights reserved. Reproduction in any form or by any means is strictly prohibited without the written consent of the author and the publisher, and their successors.

Lionel and Lionel Trains are trademarks of Lionel Trains, LLC. This book is neither authorized nor approved by Lionel Trains, LLC.

Greenberg Publishing is a registered trademark of *Kalmbach Publishing Co*.

First Edition

ISBN: 0-9710225-2-6

Library of Congress Control Number: 2002095327

✳ Table of Contents ✳

CHAPTER 1 *Introduction* *1-1*

  Foreword *1-1*
  Acknowledgments *1-3*
  References *1-4*
  Parts *1-5*

CHAPTER 2 *Motorized Units* *2-1*

  The #41 Army Turbine *2-2*
  The #42 Picatinny Arsenal *2-2*
  The #44 Missile Launcher Motor *2-5*
  The #45 Missile Launcher Motor *2-5*
  The #50 Section Gang Car Motor *2-19*
  The #51 Navy Yard Switcher *2-2*
  The #52 Fire Car Motor *2-8*
  The #53 Rio Grande Snowplow *2-2*
  The #54 Ballast Tamper Car *2-10*
  The #55 Tie-Jector Car *2-2*
  The #56 Minneapolis & St. Louis Switcher *2-2*
  The #57 A. E. C. Switcher *2-2*
  The #58 Rotary Snowplow *2-12*
  The #59 Minuteman Switcher *2-2*
  The #60 Trolley *2-13*
  The #65 Motorized Handcar Motor *2-15*
  The #68 Inspection Car (Postwar) *2-16*
  The #69 Motorized Maintenance Car Motor *2-19*

CHAPTER 3 *Bell, Whistle & Horn Units* *3-1*

  The #2403B Bell Tender Mechanism *3-4*
  The WS-75 Whistle *3-5*
  The WS-125/WS-175 et al. Whistle(s) *3-7*

✳ *Table of Contents* ✳

CHAPTER 4 *Rolling Stock* *4-1*

    The #3356 Horse Car *4-3*
    The #3359 Twin Bin Dump Car *4-4*
    The #3361 Lumber Dump Car *4-4*
    The #3360 Burro Crane Motor *4-5*
    The #3366 Corral *4-7*
    The #3366 Circus Car *4-7*
    The #3424 Operating Brakeman Car *4-8*
    The #3435 Aquarium Car *4-9*
    The #3444 Animated Gondola *4-10*
    The #3451 Lumber Car *4-11*
    The #3461 Operating Lumber Car *4-11*
    The #3454 Merchandise Car *4-12*
    The #3459 Automatic Dump Car *4-13*
    The #3469 Ore Dump Car *4-13*
    The #3462 Milk Car *4-14*
    The #3472 ('49) Milk Car *4-14*
    The #3472 Milk Car *4-15*
    The #3482 Milk Car *4-16*
    The #3520 Searchlight Coil *4-17*
    The #3620 Searchlight Coil *4-17*
    The #3530 Generator Car *4-18*
    The #3535 Security Car *4-19*
    The #3559 Dump Car *4-20*
    The #3562 Operating Barrel Car *4-21*
    The #3656 Stock Car & Platform *4-22*
    The #3662 Milk Car *4-25*
    The #3672 Bosco Milk Car *4-25*
    The #3927 Track Cleaning Car *4-26*

CHAPTER 5 *Accessories* *5-1*

    The #30 Water Tower *5-2*
    The #38 Water Tower *5-2*
    The #45 Gateman *5-5*
    The #45N Automatic Gateman *5-5*

✳ Table of Contents ✳

The #97 Coal Elevator	5-6
The #164 Lumber Loader	5-6
The #128 Animated Newsstand	5-11
The #138 Water Tower	5-12
The #140 Banjo Signal	5-13
The #145 Automatic Gateman	5-14
The #1047 Switchman	5-14
The #151 Semaphore ('51)	5-15
The #151 Semaphore ('54/'59)	5-16
The #152 Crossing Gate	5-17
The #155 Ringing Signal	5-18
The #161 Mailbag Pickup	5-19
The #182 Remote Magnet Crane	5-20
The #175 Rocket Launcher	5-24
The #192 Control Tower	5-26
The #197 Radar Tower	5-27
The #252 Crossing Gate	5-28
The #262 Automatic Highway Crossing Signal	5-29
The #264 Lumber Unloader	5-30
The #282 Portal Gantry Crane	5-31
The #282R Gantry Crane	5-31
The #299 Code Transmitter Set	5-37
The #313 Bascule Bridge Motor	5-38
The #334 Operating Dispatch Board	5-40
The #342 Culvert Pipe Loader	5-41
The #345 Culvert Pipe Unloader	5-42
The #350 Transfer Table Motor	5-43
The #497 Coaling Station Motor	5-43
The #352 Icing Station	5-47
The #356 Operating Freight Station	5-48
The #362 Barrel Loader	5-49
The #364 Lumber Loader Motor	5-50
The #397 Coal Loader Motor	5-50
The #375 Turntable	5-53
The #415 Fueling Station	5-54
The #445 Switch Tower	5-55

✶ Table of Contents ✶

The #455 Operating Oil Derrick *5-56*
The #456 Coal Ramp Set *5-57*
The #464 Operating Lumber Mill *5-58*
The #494 Rotary Beacon *5-59*
The #1045 Automatic Crossing Watchman *5-60*

CHAPTER 6   *Remote Control Track & Switches* *6-1*

The #022 Remote Control Switch *6-2*
The #37 Uncoupling Section *6-4*
The #112 Remote Control Switch *6-5*
The #112-1 Super O Switches *6-5*
The #112R Super O Switches *6-5*
The #1121 O27 Switch *6-6*
The #1122 027 Remote Control Switch Coils *6-7*
The #6009 Remote Control Track Coil *6-8*
The #6019 Remote Control Track Section Coil *6-8*
The #6029 Remote Control Track Coil *6-8*
The UCS Remote Control Track *6-9*

CHAPTER 7   *Troubleshooting & Repair* *7-1*

Motorized Units *7-2*
Whistles *7-7*
Accessories *7-9*
The "Vibrotor" Motor *7-10*
The "String & Spring" Motor *7-11*
Repairability Issues *7-13*

CHAPTER 8   *Conclusion* *8-1*

Summary *8-1*
Support *8-3*

❋ Part Number Index ❋

37-11 (Coil Assy) 6-4	140-19 (Coil) 5-13
38P-1 (Pump Motor) 5-3	145-5 (Coil) 5-14
38P-11 (Armature) 5-3	151-55 ('51 Coil) 5-15
41-28 (Field) 2-11	152-4 (Coil) 5-17
41-28 (Field) 2-4	155-10 (Coil) 5-18
41-28 (Field) 4-27	161-11 (Coil & Bracket) . . . 5-19
41-40 (Armature) 2-13	164-13 (Coil) 5-10
41-40 (Armature) 2-3	165-39 (Solenoid) 5-23
44-101 (Motor) 2-5	165M-1 (Motor) 5-20
44-6 (Coil) 2-7	165M-8 (Armature) 5-20
50-42 (Field) 2-14	175-100 (Motor Coil) 5-24
50-42 (Field) 2-20	175-8 (Coil) 5-25
50-50 (Armature) 2-19	182-29 (Magnet) 5-22
52-33 (Armature) 2-8	192-31 (Motor) 5-26
52-48 (Field) 2-9	197-26 (Motor) 5-27
54-4 (Motor) 2-10	252-52 (Coil) 5-28
54-40 (Postwar Armature) 2-10	262-64 (Coil) 5-29
58-14 (Chassis) 2-12	264-101 (Motor) 5-30
60-65 (Chassis) 2-13	282-100 (Motor) 5-31
65-201 (Motor) 2-15	282-106 (Armature) 5-32
65-202 (Armature) 2-15	282-156 (Clutch Solenoid) . 5-35
68-100 (Postwar Motor) . . 2-17	282-20 (Clutch Solenoid) . . 5-34
68-22 (Postwar Field) 2-18	282-300 (Motor) 5-31
68-26 (Postwar Armature) 2-17	282-65 (Electromagnet) . . . 5-36
97-21 (Coil) 5-9	299-19 (Coil) 5-37
97-9 (Coil) 5-8	313M-1 (Motor) 5-38
97M-1 (Motor) 5-6	313M-10 (Armature) 5-38
97M-6 (Armature) 5-6	334-40 (Motor) 5-40
112-100 RH (Coil) 6-5	342-106 (Coil) 5-41
112-101 LH (Coil) 6-5	345-117 (Motor) 5-42
112-229 RH (Coil) 6-5	350-100 (Motor) 5-43
112-230 LH (Coil) 6-5	352-33 (Coil) 5-47
114-55 (Horn) 3-3	356-50 (Coil) 5-48
128-15 (Motor) 5-11	362-20 (Coil) 5-49
138-18 (Coil) 5-5	364M-1 (Motor) 5-50
138-23 (Coil) 5-12	364M-5 (Armature) 5-44

✻ *Part Number Index* ✻

364M-5 (Armature) 5-51	3435-7 (Coil) 4-9
375-27 (Motor). 5-53	3444-29 (Coil) 4-10
397M-1 (Motor) 5-50	3451-32 (Coil) 4-11
415-40 (Coil) 5-54	3451-72 (Coil) 4-13
445-10 (Coil) 5-55	3454-13 (Coil) 4-12
455-64 (Coil) 5-56	3462-81 (Coil) 4-14
456-54 (Coil) 5-57	3472-37 (Coil) 4-15
464-45 (Motor). 5-58	3482-14 (Coil) 4-16
494-40 (Coil) 5-59	3520-20 (Coil) 4-17
497-200 (Motor). 5-43	3530-46 (Coil) 4-18
497-44 (Chute Coil) 5-46	3535-7 (Coil) 4-19
58-22 (Armature) 2-12	362-22 (Coil) 4-21
711-127 ('54+ Coil) 6-3	3652-30 (Coil in #164) 5-10
711-127 ('54/'59 Coil) 5-16	3652-30 (Coil) 5-2
711-163 Switch Motor 6-2	3656-138 ('49 Coil) 4-23
711-202 ('49 & '50 Coil) . . . 6-2	3656-185 (Coil) 4-24
1045-13 (Coil & Bracket) . . 5-60	3656-189 ('50-'54 Coil) . . . 4-24
1045-5 (Coil). 5-60	3656-28 (Coil) 4-22
1055-118 (Armature) 2-5	3662-66 (Coil) 4-25
1121-27 (Coil). 6-6	3859-17 (Coil & Leads) . . . 4-20
1122-198 6-7	3859-5 (Coil) 4-20
1122-199 6-7	3927-11 (Armature) 4-26
1122-54 6-7	6019-31 (Coil) 6-8
1122-54X. 6-7	UCS-11 (Coil). 6-9
1122-55 6-7	WS-101 (Armature) 3-5
1122-55X. 6-7	WS-125 3-7
2227B-7 (Bell Solenoid) 3-4	WS-135 3-7
2367-55 (Horn) 3-3	WS-149 3-7
3356-24 (Coil). 4-3	WS-175 3-7
3356-47 (Coil). 4-7	WS-181 3-7
3360-36 (Armature) 4-5	WS-200. 3-2
3360-44 (Field) 4-6	WS-250 3-3
3361-16 (Coil). 4-4	WS-75 3-5
3424-25 (Coil). 4-8	

✻ *Unit Number Index* ✻

# 30 Water Tower 5-2	# 152 Crossing Gate. 5-17
# 37 Uncoupling Section . . . 6-4	# 155 Ringing Signal 5-18
# 38 Water Tower 5-2	# 161 Mailbag Pickup 5-19
# 41 Army Turbine 2-2	# 175 Rocket Launcher 5-24
# 42 Picatinny Arsenal 2-2	# 182 Remote Magnet Crane 5-20
# 44 Missile Launcher 2-5	# 192 Control Tower 5-26
# 45 Gateman 5-5	# 197 Radar Tower 5-27
# 45 Missile Launcher 2-5	# 252 Crossing Gate 5-28
# 45N Gateman 5-5	# 257 Freight Station 3-3
# 50 Section Gang Car 2-19	# 262 Highway Signal 5-29
# 51 Navy Yard Switcher . . 2-2	# 264 Lumber Unloader 5-30
# 52 Fire Car 2-8	# 282 Portal Gantry Crane . . 5-31
# 53 Snowplow 2-2	# 282R Gantry Crane 5-31
# 54 Ballast Tamper 2-10	# 299 Code Transmitter Set . 5-37
# 55 Tie-Jector 2-2	# 313 Bascule Bridge 5-38
# 56 M&StL Switcher 2-2	# 334 Op. Dispatch Board . . 5-40
# 57 A.E.C. Switcher 2-2	# 342 Culvert Pipe Loader . . 5-41
# 58 Rotary Snowplow . . . 2-12	# 345 Culvert Pipe Unloader 5-42
# 59 Minuteman Switcher . . 2-2	# 350 Transfer Table 5-43
# 60 Trolley 2-13	# 352 Icing Station 5-47
# 65 Motorized Handcar . . 2-15	# 356 Op. Freight Station . . . 5-48
# 68 Inspection Car ('58-'61) 2-17	# 362 Barrel Loader 5-49
# 69 Maintenance Car 2-19	# 364 Lumber Loader 5-50
# 97 Coal Elevator 5-6	# 375 Turntable 5-53
# 022 Switch 6-2	# 397 Coal Loader 5-50
# 112 Switch 6-5	# 415 Fueling Station 5-54
# 112-1 Super O Switch 6-5	# 445 Switch Tower 5-55
# 112R Super O Switch 6-5	# 455 Oil Derrick 5-56
# 114 Newsstand (w/Horn) . . 3-3	# 456 Coal Ramp Set 5-57
# 118 Newsstand Whistle . . . 3-3	# 464 Op. Lumber Mill 5-58
# 128 Animated Newsstand 5-11	# 494 Rotary Beacon 4-17
# 138 Water Tower 5-12	# 494 Rotary Beacon 5-59
# 140 Banjo Signal 5-13	# 494 Rotary Beacon 5-59
# 145 Automatic Gateman . 5-14	# 497 Coaling Station 5-43
# 151 Semaphore ('51) 5-15	#1047 Switchman 5-14
# 151 Semaphore ('54/'59). 5-16	#1047 Switchman 5-60

✻ Unit Number Index ✻

#1121 Switch. 6-6	#3472 Milk Car. 4-15
#1122 Switch 6-7	#3482 Milk Car. 4-16
#2403B (Bell Tender) 3-4	#3520 Searchlight Coil. . . . 4-17
#3356 Horse Car 4-3	#3530 Generator Car 4-18
#3359 Twin Bin Dump Car. . 4-4	#3535 Security Car. 4-19
#3360 Burro Crane 4-5	#3559 Dump Car 4-20
#3361 Lumber Dump Car . . . 4-4	#3562 Op. Barrel Car 4-21
#3366 Circus Car. 4-7	#3620 Searchlight Coil. . . . 4-17
#3366 Corral 4-7	#3656 Platform ('49) 4-23
#3424 Operating Brakeman . 4-8	#3656 Stock Car ('49) 4-22
#3435 Aquarium Car. 4-9	#3656 Stock Car ('50-'54) . 4-24
#3444 Animated Gondola . . 4-10	#3662 Milk Car. 4-25
#3451 Lumber Car 4-11	#3672 Bosco Milk Car 4-25
#3454 Merchandise Car . . . 4-12	#3927 Track Cleaning Car . 4-26
#3459 Automatic Dump Car 4-13	#6009 RC Track Section. . . . 6-8
#3461 Operating Lumber Car 4-11	#6019 Track Section. 6-8
#3462 Milk Car. 4-14	#6029 RC Track Section. . . . 6-8
#3469 Ore Dump Car 4-13	All Whistles ('48+). 3-7
#3472 ('49) Milk Car 4-14	UCS Remote Control Track . 6-9

O-Gauge - Lionel POSTWAR Reference Manual   x

CHAPTER 1 *Introduction*

✱ *Foreword* ✱

This is the second volume dealing with the electrical components of Postwar Lionel O-Gauge trains. The focus of this volume is to provide complete coverage of the small motors and coils used in Motorized Units, Whistles, Rolling Stock and Accessories. It also includes information on the coils used in Switches and Control Sections.

Motorized Units

This manual provides complete coverage of the wound components used in these units. The units were produced between 1954 and 1966. The "Troubleshooting" section provides information on widely available replacement parts which will extend the life of these units.

Whistles

Not that complicated when you realize there were only two basic types of whistle motors: the diecast whistle and the plastic whistle. If the windings are still viable, these tough little motors can often be restored to original operating condition.

Rolling Stock & Accessories

A wide range of operating cars, dump cars, and their related platforms, with an amazing array of technologies ranging from buzzers and solenoids, to very large O-Gauge motors. This manual also provides complete coverage of all vibrating "motors" used in these products.

Continuing the approach started in Volume I, every entry in this manual emphasizes Component Recognition, Troubleshooting, and Repair.

Component Recognition

 Component recognition is especially important in Motorized Units and Whistles. Recognition of the commutator pitch, fractional differences in the length of the shaft and, in some cases, the "cut" of the worm gear on the end of the armature shaft is very important for these units.

Troubleshooting

 Troubleshooting, defined as the simple act of inspecting a component, taking a measurement or set of measurements with an ohmmeter, and then comparing the reading(s) to the entries in this manual, is as simple as using a digital thermometer. The meter does all the work for you.

Repair

 The information in this manual supports a broad spectrum of repair activities, ranging from simple inspection to cleaning, lubricating, re-soldering, and even rebuilding coils. An expanded Troubleshooting & Repair section provides simple tips and references to help you rejuvenate those "tired" operating assemblies.

It is no secret that availability of wound replacement parts has fallen way behind availability of mechanical or ornamental parts. You can use the notes in the "Troubleshooting" section to prevent further damage to the wound components in the units you have. For those units which have been pushed too far, you now have the information, and the support, needed to have them repaired or rebuilt!

✳ ✳ ✳
✳ *Acknowledgments* ✳

Completion of this manual could not have been accomplished without the invaluable assistance of Messrs. Jeff Kane and Richard Smith. Both maintain extensive inventories of reasonably-priced parts, and are known for their initiative in having obscure, but operationally-critical, parts reproduced. Both are also known for their extremely high-level of customer service and support.

But most astounding was the amount of personal time they were willing to contribute to the completion of this manual. Contact information on these individuals is provided later in this chapter.

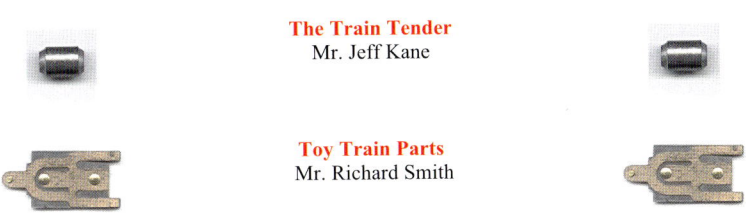

The Train Tender
Mr. Jeff Kane

Toy Train Parts
Mr. Richard Smith

The following individuals provided what can only be called a last-minute save. This manual would not have gone to print without their "11th Hour" contribution(s).

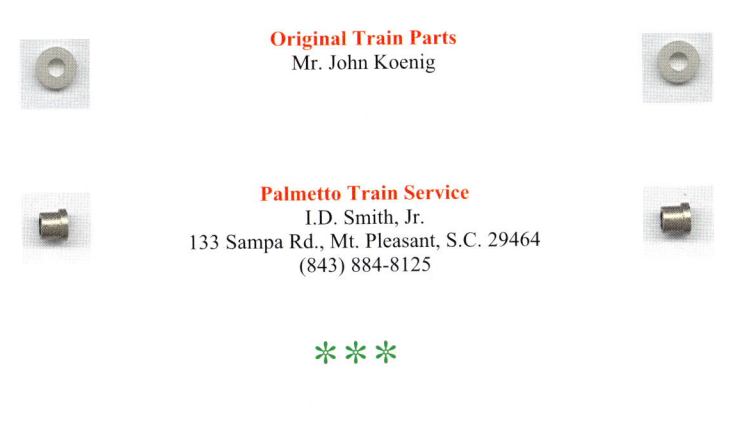

Original Train Parts
Mr. John Koenig

Palmetto Train Service
I.D. Smith, Jr.
133 Sampa Rd., Mt. Pleasant, S.C. 29464
(843) 884-8125

✳ ✳ ✳

O-Gauge - Lionel POSTWAR Reference Manual 1-3

✳✳✳
✳ References ✳

The "part number" information on wound components was obtained, cross-checked, and confirmed using the following references. Any of these manuals can be used in conjunction with the unique material contained in this manual to locate the motor, armature or coil number of the unit you are trying to identify or repair. These references provide the mechanical & ornamental breakdowns of the units referenced in this manual.

- *Lionel Factory Bulletins and Exploded Parts* lists, 1946 - 1969 (Scattered & Miscellaneous, and in various states of completeness).

- *Greenberg's Repair and Operating Manual For Lionel Trains*, 1945-1969, Pauker and Greenberg, Greenberg Books/Division of Kalmbach Publishing Co., ISBN: 0-89778-040-X, 1990.

- *Complete Service Manual for Lionel Trains*, K-Line (MDK, Inc.), Copyright 1978 by Aurotech, Inc.; Reprinted 1998 by MDK, Inc.

- *Greenberg's Lionel Service Manual*, I.D. Smith, 4-Volume Set, ISBN: 89778-019-1, Copyright 1984.

The following references describe Lionel production from 1945-1969. Volume VI will prove especially useful as many of the entries contain descriptions of the operating characteristics of the accessories.

- *Greenberg's Lionel Trains, 1945-1969*; Volume I; Motive Power and Rolling Stock; Ninth Edition; 1996; ISBN: 0-89778-503-7; Paul V. Ambrose; Kalmbach Publishing Co., 21027 Crossroads Circle, Waukesha, WI 53187; http://kalmbachbooks.com.

- *Greenberg's Lionel Trains, 1945-1969*; Volume VI: Accessories; Second Edition; 2001; ISBN: 0-89778-475-8 (soft); ISBN: 0-89778-476-6 (Hard); Alan Stewart; Kalmbach Publishing Co., 21027 Crossroads Circle, Waukesha, WI 53187; http://kalmbachbooks.com.

✳ ✳ ✳
✳ *Parts* ✳

Without a doubt, the world of Lionel trains enjoys the widest available line of replacement parts in the world. In some cases, parts going back 40 or more years are still available. There are several reasons for this.

The first reason has been production of parts by Lionel to support manufacturing of its products and to supply spares to its network of authorized Service Stations.

A second reason is that Lionel reused selected parts in the production of later models. This further extended the availability of certain parts.

A third reason is the reproduction of parts when certain pieces were no longer available from the factory, or the fact that many pieces continued to be available from industrial supply sources (e.g, rivets, bearings, etc.).

A fourth reason is the salvaging of parts from severely damaged locos and accessories.

So, if you're looking for a part, the following list is a good place to start.

✳ ✳ ✳

O-Gauge - Lionel POSTWAR Reference Manual   1-5

✳ ✳ ✳

The Train Tender
Mr. Jeff Kane
135 Hampton Way
Penfield, NY 14526-1523
(585) 381-0705
jeff@ttender.com
http://www.ttender.com

Toy Train Parts,
Mr. Richard Smith
245 Cherry Hill Parkway
Mt. Washington, KY 40047
(502) 538-7311
http://www.trainexchange.com/ttp.htm

George's Train House
George & Nancy Tebolt
Box 149
Spencertown, NY 12165
(518) 392-2660
http://www.georgetebolt.com

Dr. Tinker
Mr. Dave Laughridge
One Belfry Terrace
Lexington, MA 02421
(781) 862-5798
http://www.tttrains.com/drtinker

Charlie's Trains
Charles Clarke
P.O. Box 158
Hubertus, WI 53033
(262) 628-1544

✳ ✳ ✳

✳ ✳ ✳

Hobby Surplus Sales
Peter & Steve Amato
287 Main St.
New Britain, CT 06050
(860) 223-0600
http://www.TrainRepairParts.com

Olsens Toy Train Parts
Sal & Sharon Olsen
1390 Bonnieview
Lakewood, OH 44107
(216) 226-0444
http://www.olsenstoy.com

Stan Orr Train Parts
Stan Orr
P.O. Box 97
Stormville, NY 12582
(845) 221-7738
http://www.stanorrtrainparts.com

Ted Nyerges
580 Humiston Dr.
Bay Village, OH 44140
(440) 331-1649

French's Trains & Hobbies, Inc.
George Stanton
30-1/2 N. Dundalk Ave.
Dundalk, MD 21222
(410) 285-5809
http://www.frenchstrains.com

Original Train Parts
John Koenig
236 Grange St.
Franklin Square, NY 11010
(516) 486-6658

✳ ✳ ✳

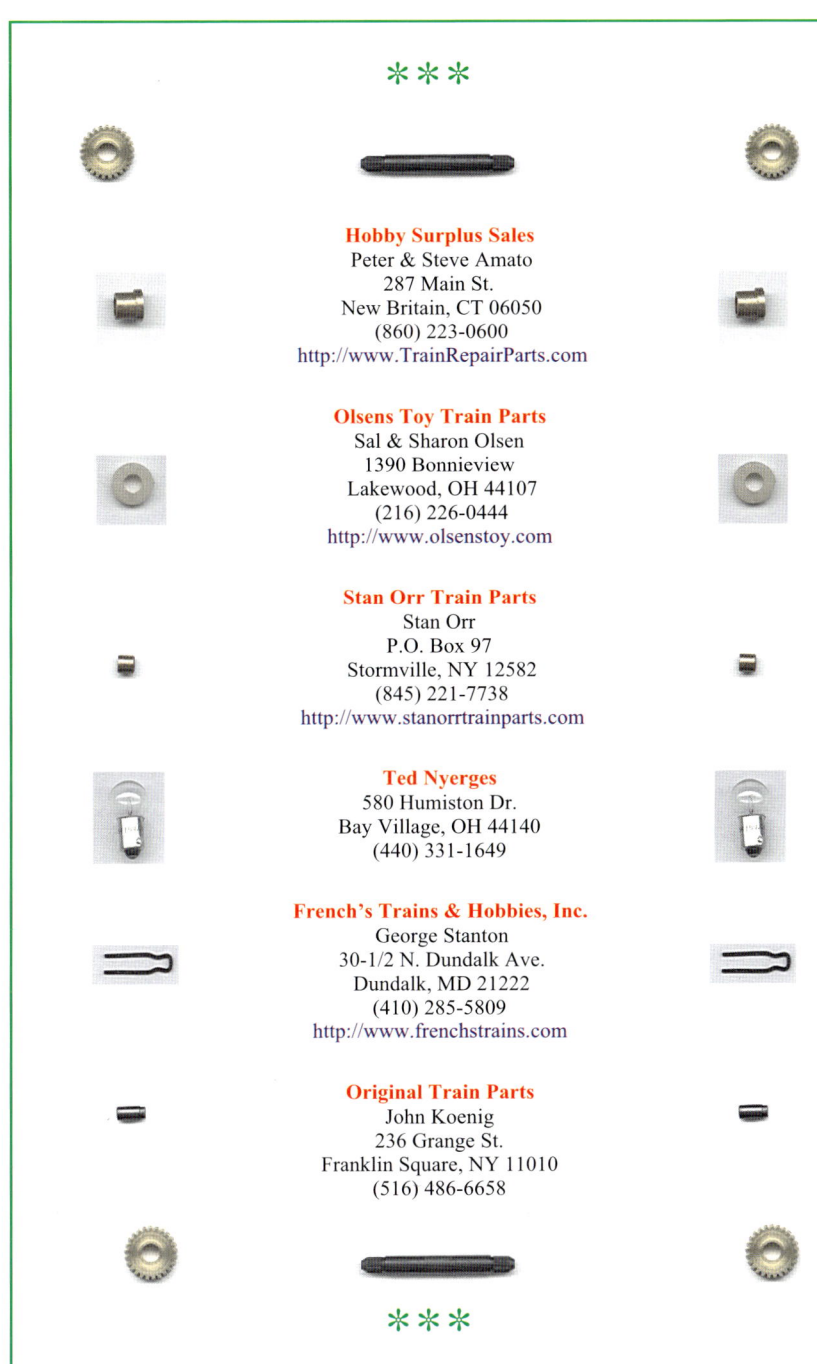

CHAPTER 2 *Motorized Units*

The following table provides a list of the units covered in this chapter, their dates of production, and their configurations. Note the heavy reuse of the 41-40 armature and the 41-28 field.

Dates	Unit	Motor	Armature	Field	Reverse
55	41	41-72	41-40	41-28	100-6
56-57	41	41-80	41-40	41-28	100-6
57	42	41-80	41-40	41-28	100-6
56-57	51	41-80	41-40	41-28	100-6
58	56	41-80	41-40	41-28	100-6
57-60	53	41-80	41-40	41-28	100-6
59-60	57	41-80	41-40	41-28	100-6
62-63	59	41-80	41-40	41-28	100-6
57-61	55	41-80	41-40	41-28	None
59-62	44	44-101	1055-118		100-11
60-62	45	44-101	1055-118		100-11
58-61	52	52-42	52-33	52-48	Mech.
59-61	58	58-14	58-22	41-28	100-6
54-64	50	50-96	50-50	50-42	Mech.
60-62	69	50-96	50-50	50-42	Mech
58-61	54	54-4	54-40	41-28	None
55-58	60	60-65	41-40	50-42	Mech
62-66	65	65-201	65-202		None
58-61	68	68-100	68-26	68-22	101-2

Just a few of the units covered in this section. See Chapter 7 for some very useful tips on evaluating and repairing these units.

✱ The #41 Army Turbine ✱
✱ The #42 Picatinny Arsenal ✱
✱ The #51 Navy Yard Switcher ✱
✱ The #53 Rio Grande Snowplow ✱
✱ The #55 Tie-Jector Car ✱
✱ The #56 Minneapolis & St. Louis Switcher ✱
✱ The #57 A. E. C. Switcher ✱
✱ The #59 Minuteman Switcher ✱

All of these units used the 41-40 Armature, and the 41-28 Field.

1955 Production: (Chassis #41-72)

From a #41 Switcher

1956 Production: (Chassis #41-80)

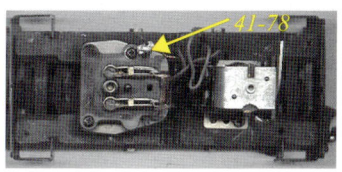

From a #51 Switcher

The Tie-Jector Chassis of 1958

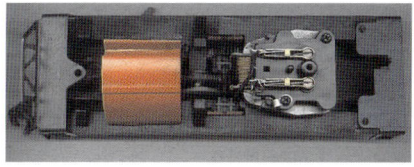
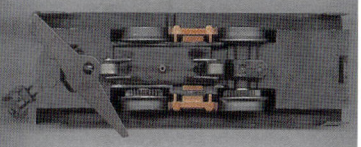

The Motorized Unit Armature (41-40)

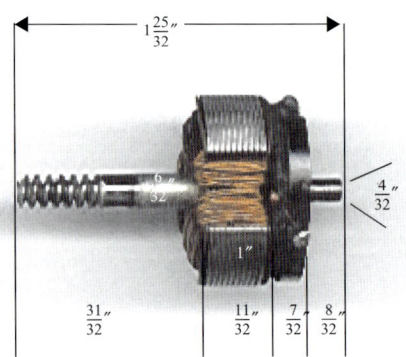

Motor Detail	Specifications	
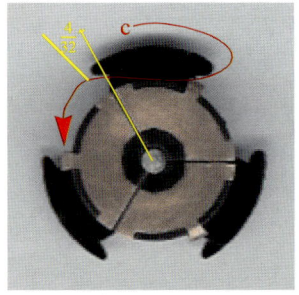	Wire Size:	27 (0.0130)
	# of Turns:	58
	Style:	Layered
	# of Layers:	6
	Direction:	Clockwise
	Resistance :	1.1 - 1.2 Ω
	Tie-Off:	Common

The Motorized Unit Field (41-28)

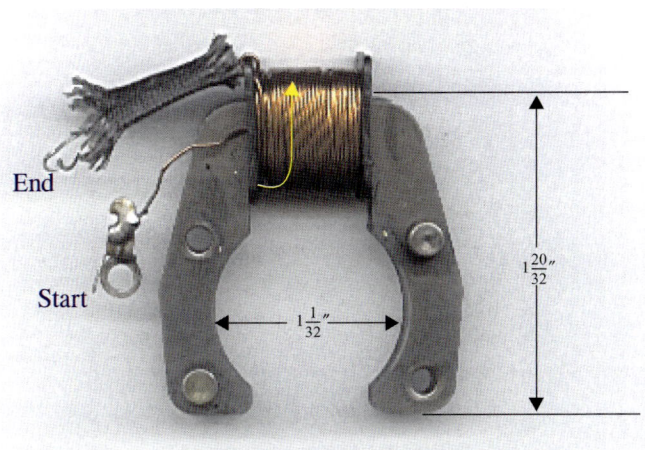

End

Start

$1\frac{1}{32}"$

$1\frac{20}{32}"$

Component Detail	Specifications	
101-6 RCU	Wire Size:	24 (0.0191)
	# of Turns:	132 - 141
	Style:	Layered
	# of Layers:	6
	Resistance:	.9 - 1.0 Ω
	Thickness:	11/32"

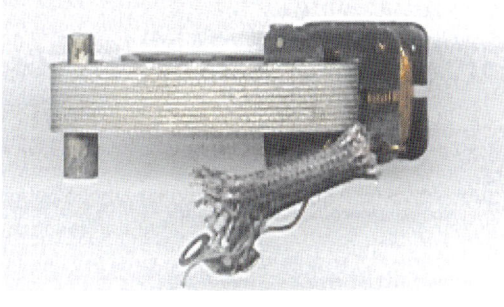

✻ *The #44 Missile Launcher Motor* ✻
✻ *The #45 Missile Launcher Motor* ✻

The #44/#45 Armature (1055-118)

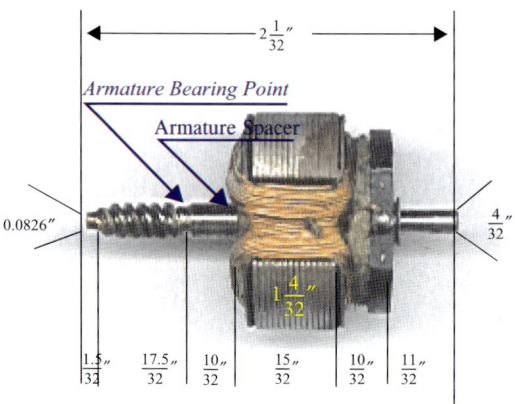

Note: Shown with CON-8 Washer and 600-129 Thrust washer set.

Motor Detail	Specifications	
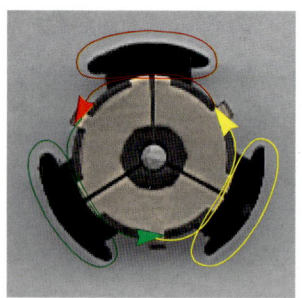	*Wire Size:*	28 (0.0118)
	# of Turns:	129
	Style:	Layered
	# of Layers:	10
	Direction:	Clockwise
	Resistance :	1.3 - 1.4 Ω
	Tie-Off:	End-To-End

The #44/#45 Field

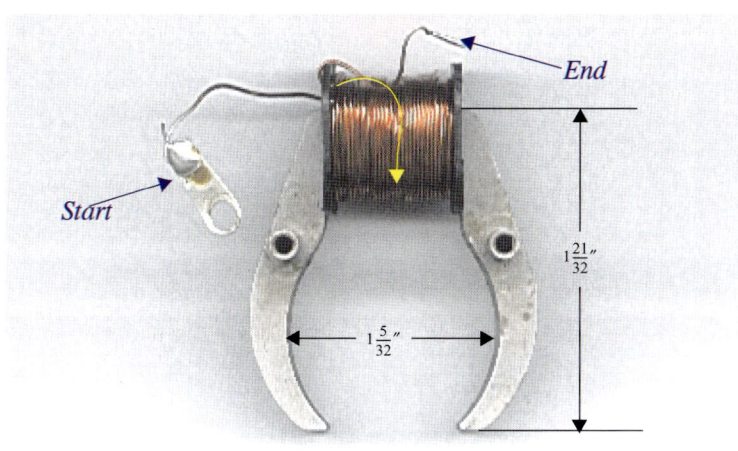

Motor Detail	Specifications	
	Wire Size:	24 (0.0194)
	# of Turns:	151
	Style:	Layered
	# of Layers:	6
	Resistance:	1.1 Ω
	Thickness:	15.5/32"

The #44/#45 Missile Firing Coil (44-6)

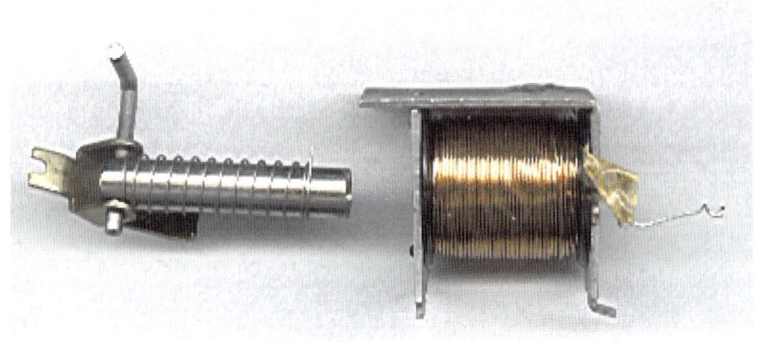

Motor Detail	Specifications	
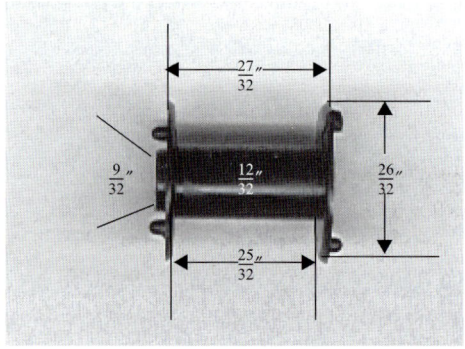	Wire Size:	26 (0.0154)
	# of Turns:	501
	Style:	Layered
	# of Layers:	12
	Resistance :	3.4 Ω
	Thickness:	(cf. Below)

✸ *The #52 Fire Car Motor* ✸

The #52 Armature (52-33)

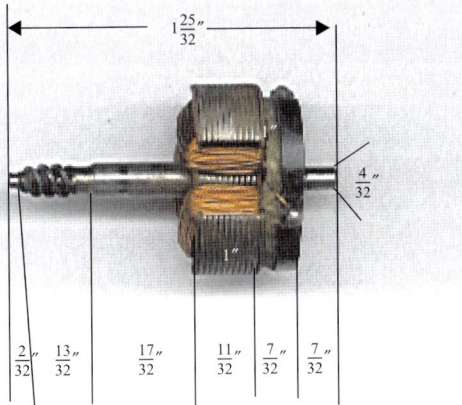

Motor Detail	Specifications	
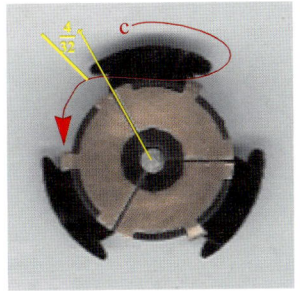	Wire Size:	27 (0.0130)
	# of Turns:	60
	Style:	Layered
	# of Layers:	6
	Direction:	Clockwise
	Resistance :	1.2 - 1.3 Ω
	Tie-Off:	Common

O-Gauge - Lionel POSTWAR Reference Manual

The #52 Field (52-48)

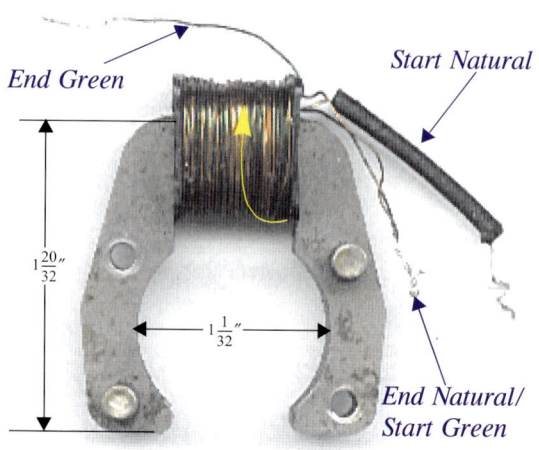

Concurrently wound double strand (Natural/Green)

Motor Detail	Specifications	
	Wire Size:	28 (0.0119)
	# of Turns:	180 (doublestrand)
	Style:	Layered
	# of Layers:	10
	Resistance :	Natural: 2.2 Ω
		Green: 2.3-2.4 Ω
	Thickness:	11/32

✳ The #54 Ballast Tamper Car ✳

The #54 Motor Armature (54-40)

Note: All samples had overtensioned #27 wire with extra turns.

Motor Detail	Specifications	
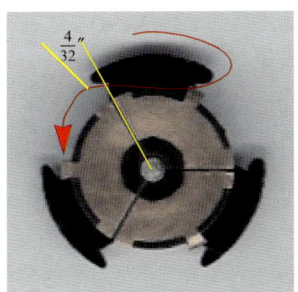	Wire Size:	27-28 (0.0129-0.0130)
	# of Turns:	67
	Style:	Layered
	# of Layers:	6
	Direction:	Clockwise
	Resistance :	1.3 - 1.4 Ω
	Tie-Off:	Common

O-Gauge - Lionel POSTWAR Reference Manual

The #54 Motor Field (41-28)

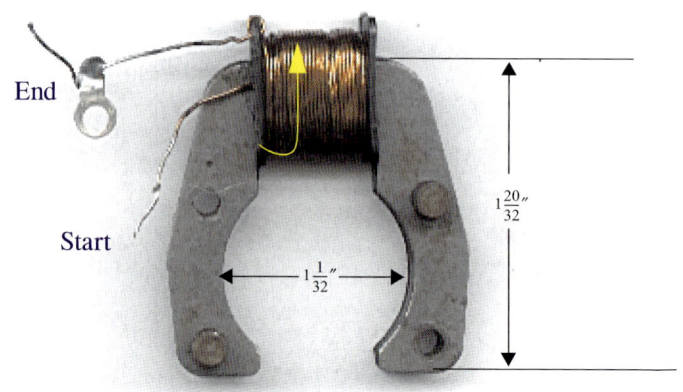

End

Start

$1\frac{1}{32}''$

$1\frac{20}{32}''$

Motor Detail	Specifications	
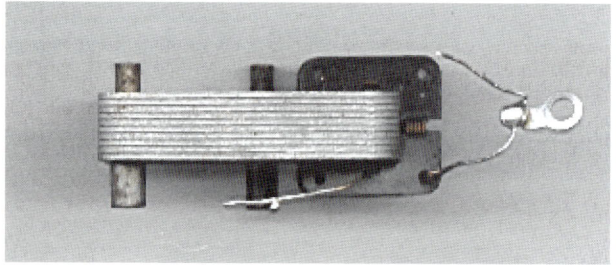	Wire Size:	24 (0.0192)
	# of Turns:	142 - 148
	Style:	Layered
	# of Layers:	6
	Resistance :	.9 Ω
	Thickness:	11/32"

✴ The #58 Rotary Snowplow ✴

The #58 Armature (58-22)

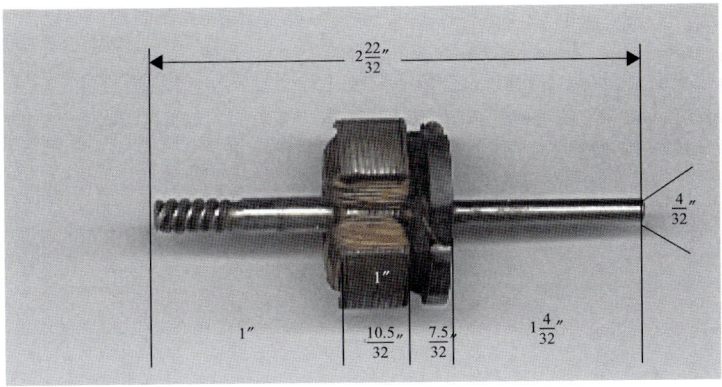

Motor Detail	Specifications	
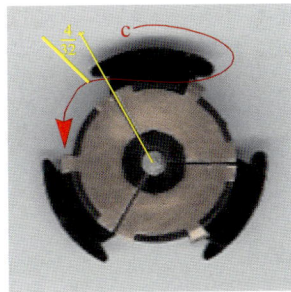	Wire Size:	27 (0.0130)
	# of Turns:	58
	Style:	Layered
	# of Layers:	6
	Direction:	Clockwise
	Resistance:	1.1 - 1.2 Ω
	Tie-Off:	Common

(Note: Double Worm)

(Note: The #58 Rotary Snowplow used the #41-28 Single Wound Field).

✻ *The #60 Trolley* ✻

The #60 Trolley Armature (41-40)

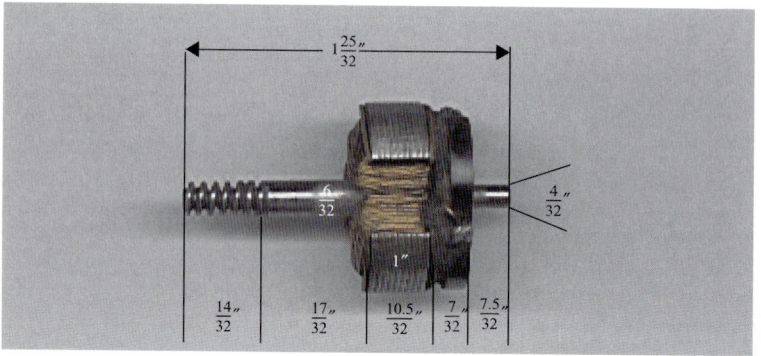

(Note: The 41-40 has a single worm)

Motor Detail	Specifications	
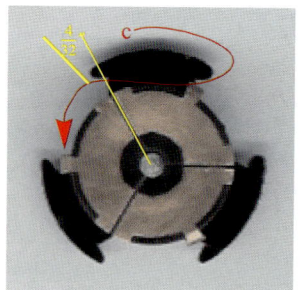	*Wire Size:*	27 (0.0131)
	# of Turns:	58
	Style:	Layered
	# of Layers:	6
	Direction:	Clockwise
	Resistance :	1.1 - 1.2 Ω
	Tie-Off:	Common

The #60 Trolley Field (50-42)

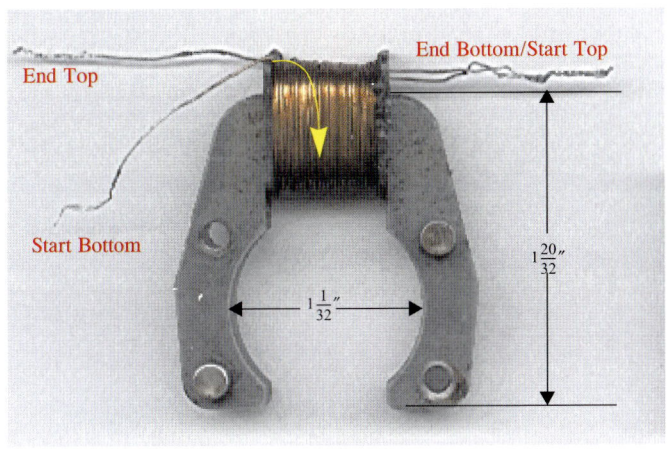

Motor Detail	Specifications	
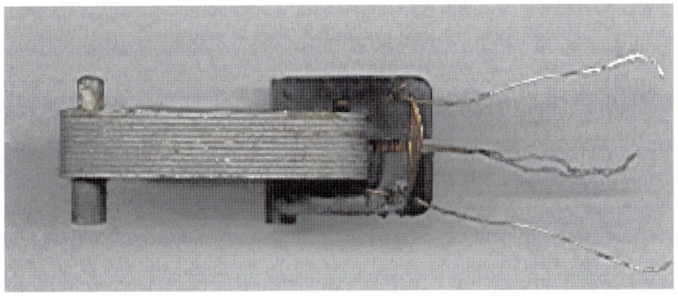	Wire Size:	28 (0.0119)
	# of Turns:	172 - 180
	Style:	Layered
	# of Layers:	10
	Resistance:	Bottom: 2.0 Ω Top: 2.3 Ω
	Thickness:	11/32"

✻ *The #65 Motorized Handcar Motor* ✻

The #65 Motorized Handcar Armature (65-202)

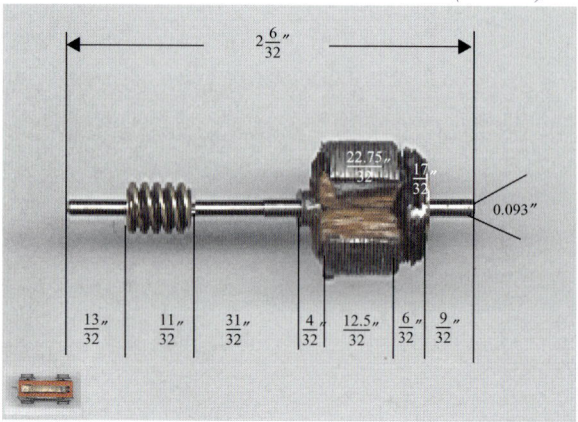

(Note: Permanent Magnet Field)

Motor Detail	Specifications	
	Wire Size:	33
	# of Turns:	150
	Style:	Layered
	# of Layers:	10
	Direction:	Clockwise
	Resistance :	2.3 Ω
	Tie-Off:	End-To-End

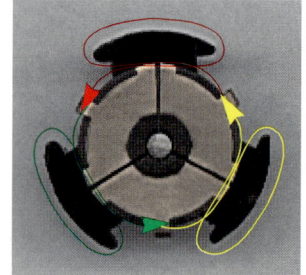

2-15 O-Gauge - Lionel Postwar Reference Manual

✻ *The #68 Inspection Car (Postwar)* ✻

Originally, produced from 1958-1961, this piece was reproduced by Lionel in the late '90s. The late '90s motor was basically the same (mechanically) with a few significant differences.

The brush plate was enhanced by an adjusting nut and an armature bearing. The wire gauge of both the armature and the field were reduced to #28 (wire colored red and green). The rear motor bearing was oversized to accommodate the splined armature shaft without damaging the bearing. Finally, The motor was equipped with a nylon pinion/spur gear for quieter operation and to minimize wear on the drive train.

The sum total of these differences resulted in a motor which ran significantly cooler in the 9-14V range, and vibrated a lot less than its postwar counterpart.

The Postwar #68 Executive Inspection Car Chassis

These comparisons were made on two, New Old Stock, motors. These motors had never been used. The reason for documenting them here is to highlight the extra attention which must be paid to periodic lubrication (as well as pickup-roller, brush plate and bearing condition) on the postwar version of the motor.

The #68 Postwar Motor Armature (68-26)

Motor Detail	Specifications	
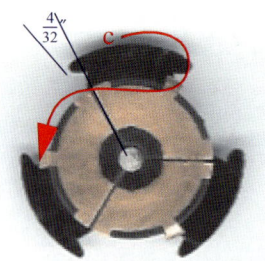	Wire Size:	27 (0.0134)
	# of Turns:	60
	Style:	Layered
	# of Layers:	6
	Direction:	Clockwise
	Resistance :	1.2 Ω
	Tie-Off:	Common

The #68 Postwar Motor Field (68-22)

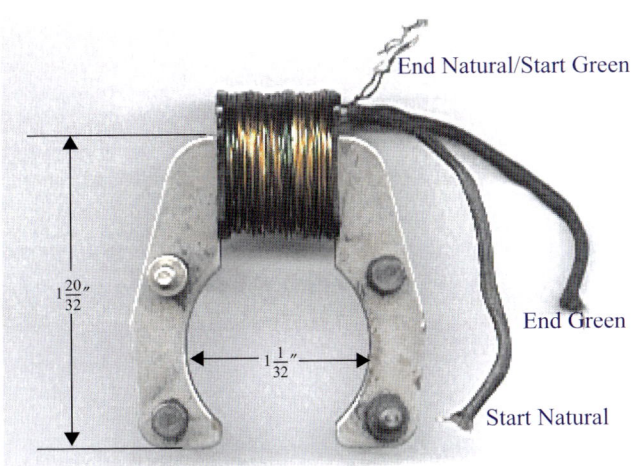

Motor Detail	Specifications	
	Wire Size:	27 (0.0137)
	# of Turns:	171
	Style:	Layered
	# of Layers:	10
Black Metal Gear	Resistance :	
	Single Strand:	1.7 - 1.8 Ω
	End-To-End:	3.4 - 3.5 Ω

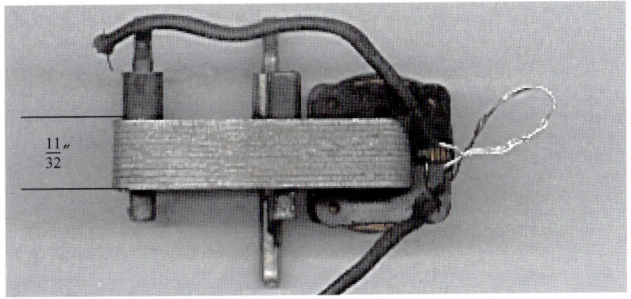

✻ The #50 Section Gang Car Motor ✻
✻ The #69 Motorized Maintenance Car Motor ✻

The #50/#69 Armature (50-50)

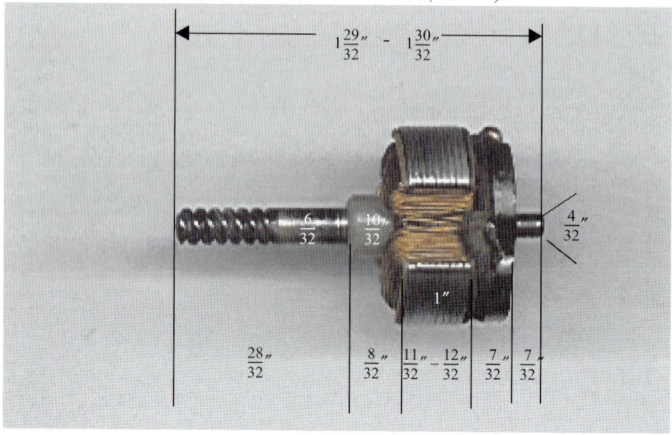

(Note: The 50-50 has a double worm)

Motor Detail	Specifications	
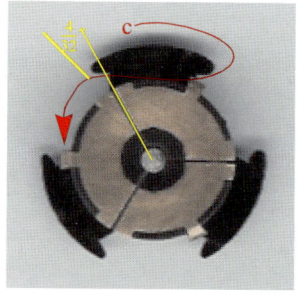 *From a #69*	Wire Size:	27 (0.0131)
	# of Turns:	60
	Style:	Layered
	# of Layers:	6
	Direction:	Clockwise
	Resistance :	1.1 Ω
	Tie-Off:	Common

The #50/#69 Field (50-42)

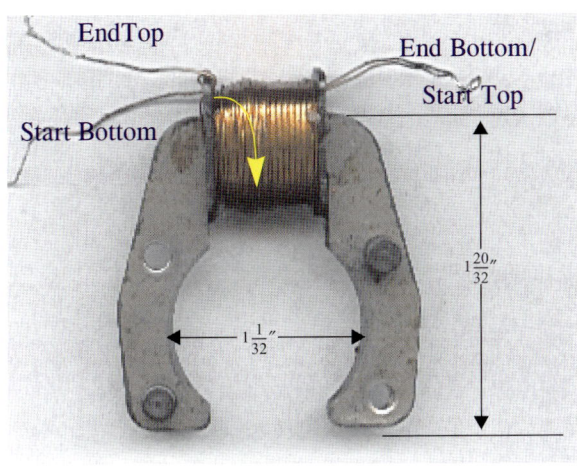

Motor Detail	Specifications	
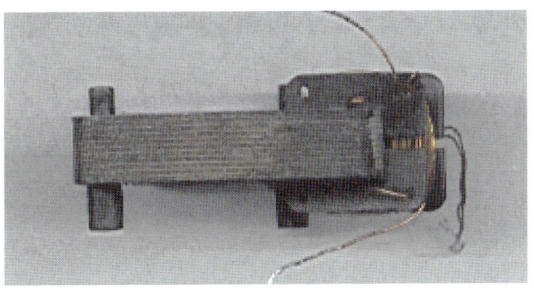 *From a #69*	Wire Size:	28 (0.0119)
	# of Turns:	Top: 185
		Bottom: 185
	Style:	Layered
	# of Layers:	5 (each coil)
	Resistance :	Top: 2.3 Ω
		Bottom: 1.9-2.0 Ω
	Thickness:	11/32"

CHAPTER 3 *Bell, Whistle & Horn Units*

Two basic types of whistle units were used in the postwar years. The first had a relatively heavy cast frame and was a carryover from the prewar years. This whistle was designed for O27 operation and was numbered the WS-75. In the postwar years, it was only used until 1948. In 1948, it was replaced by the WS-125 whistle motor and its derivatives.

Prewar Through 1948 Whistle Assemblies

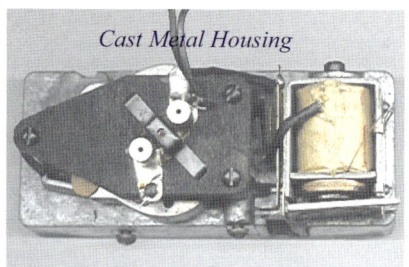

Cast Metal Housing

The WS-75 Whistle Assembly is shown with its WSR-1 Whistle Relay. The specifications on the relay are given in Volume 1.

2466WX Tender Chassis

Note

Another diecast whistle, the WS-85, was designed for O-Gauge operation. This whistle used the WS-101 armature (the same armature used in the WS-75). According to the Service Manual, this WS-85 whistle was also available from 1945 to 1948. Unexpectedly, most 1945-1948 postwar O-Gauge tenders examined had the WS-75. Those few which had the WS-85, had the prewar version of the whistle, which will be covered in the Prewar Reference Manual.

The second type of whistle had a sound chamber made from plastic. They are found in a wide variety of colors and are differentiated by how the whistle is mounted. While a huge proliferation of colors and whistle numbers resulted, the underlying whistle components (i.e., the armature and field) appear to have been consistent throughout production. The motor and impeller assembly shown above (numbered WS-135 or WS181) was the heart of the "Standard Whistle Motor" from 1948 through the end of production.

Post-1948 Whistle Assemblies

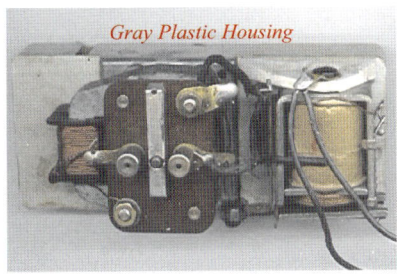
Gray Plastic Housing

The WS-125 Whistle Assembly, as found in a 6466WX Tender. This unit uses the WS-135 motor and impeller assembly (which includes the WS-149 armature). Also note that the relay is mounted on the whistle housing.

The WS-175 Whistle Assembly. As found in a 243W Tender. This unit used the WS-181 motor & impeller assembly. The relay is not mounted on the whistle body, but requires a special mounting bracket on the tender.

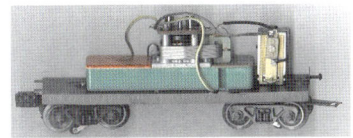

Black Plastic Housing
Double-Sided Adhesive

The WS-200 Whistle Assembly. As found in the #125 Whistle Station, this unit was secured to the bottom of the station using adhesive foam pads. This unit uses the WS-181 motor assembly.

O-Gauge - Lionel Postwar Reference Manual   3-2

Lionel reused, or adapted, several of their horn and whistle mechanisms for use in accessories. In many cases, the mounting bracket of the piece was modified. This resulted in a new part number being assigned to the component. The most notable of these "adaptations" are described in the following table. The specs and troubleshooting information for the "horn" adaptations are provided in Volume I.

Other Post-1948 Applications

The *#114 Newsstand* with electric horn. This accessory used a horn mechanism manufactured by the Delta Electric Co. of Marion, Ind. This horn was fitted directly with a holder for a 1.5 V battery.

The *#118 Newsstand Whistle*. This accessory used the standard Lionel whistle motor components of the period. Samples of this assembly with and without the oil wick cover have been seen. The configuration of the whistle in this accessory was numbered WS-250.

The *#257 Freight Station* reused the 2367-55 Horn and mounting bracket as is.

Finally, the single electrically controlled bell manufactured during the postwar years was to be found in the 2403B Bell Tender. This unit used a thermostatic/bimetallic strip to control ringing of the bell. The wound components of the bell tender were identical to their prewar 6403B counterparts.

✶ *The #2403B Bell Tender Mechanism* ✶

The #2403B Bell Solenoid (2227B-7)

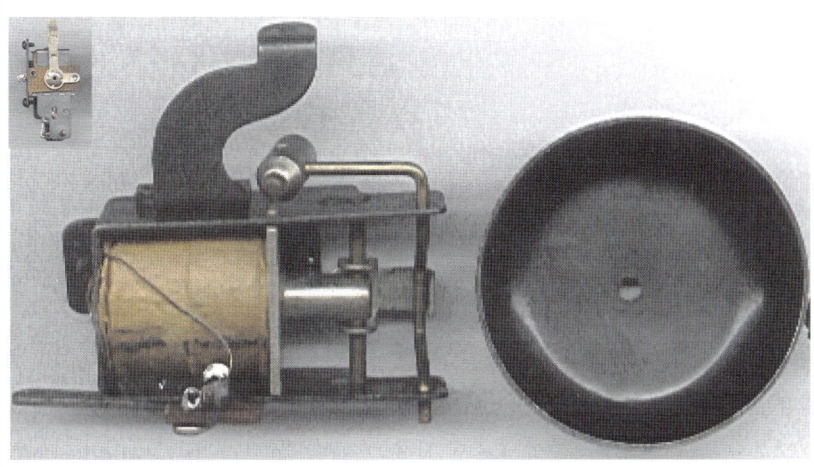

Part Detail	Specifications	
	Wire Size:	29 (0.0109)
	# of Turns:	948
	Style:	Layered
	# of Layers:	15.5
	Resistance :	12.0 - 12.1 Ω

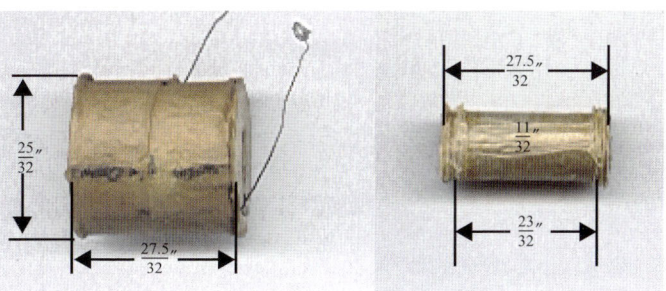

❋ *The WS-75 Whistle* ❋

The WS-75 Whistle Armature (WS-101)

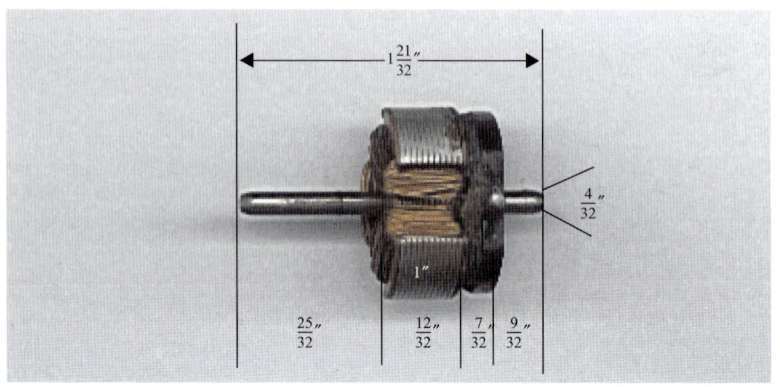

Part Detail	Specifications	
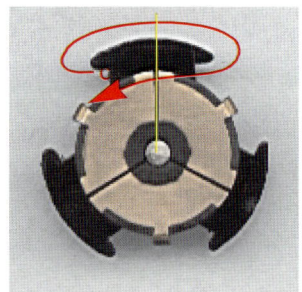	Wire Size:	27 (0.0136)
	# of Turns:	60
	Style:	Layered
	# of Layers:	6
	Direction:	Clockwise
	Resistance :	1.1 - 1.2 Ω
	Tie-Off:	Common

The WS-75 Whistle Field

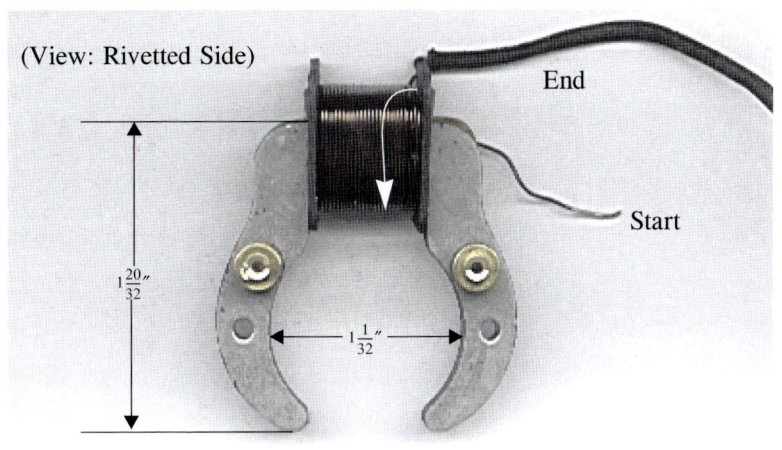

(View: Rivetted Side)

End

Start

$1\frac{20}{32}"$

$1\frac{1}{32}"$

Part Detail	Specifications	
	Wire Size:	24 (0.0195)
	# of Turns:	145
	Style:	Layered
	# of Layers:	6
	Resistance:	.9 - 1.0 Ω
	Thickness:	12/32"

✻ *The WS-125/WS-175 et al. Whistle(s)* ✻

The WS-125/WS-175 Whistle Armature (WS-149)

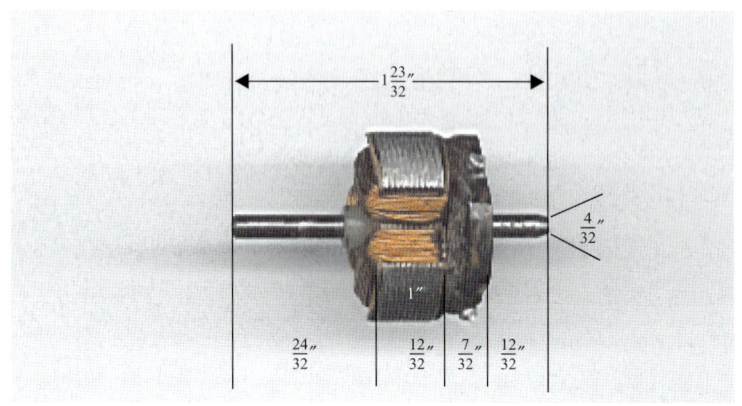

Part Detail	Specifications	
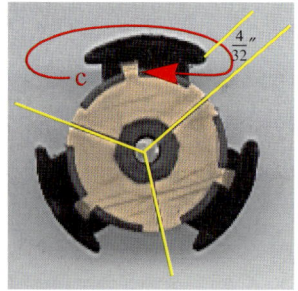	*Wire Size:*	27 (0.0137)
	# of Turns:	57-60
	Style:	Layered
	# of Layers:	6
	Direction:	Clockwise
	Resistance :	1.1 - 1.2 Ω
	Tie-Off:	Common

The WS-125/WS-175 Whistle Field

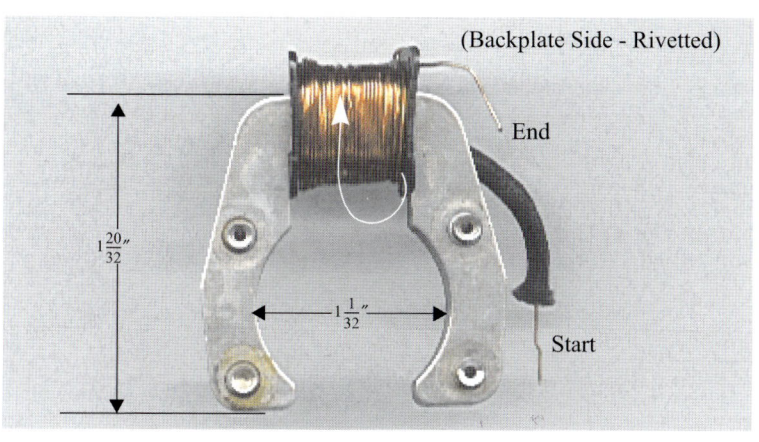

(Backplate Side - Rivetted)

End

Start

$1\frac{20}{32}"$

$1\frac{1}{32}"$

Part Detail	Specifications	
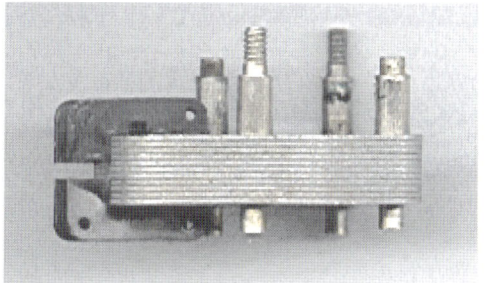	Wire Size:	24 (0.0192-0.0194)
	# of Turns:	135 - 138
	Style:	Layered
	# of Layers:	6
	Resistance :	.8 - .9 Ω
	Thickness:	10.5/32" -11/32"

CHAPTER 4 *Rolling Stock*

The cars in this section usually appear under the general heading of "Rolling Stock". But only those cars with operating coils have been included here. The coils you will see in this section range from uniquely designed solenoids, to adaptations of reverse units and vibrator motors.

Paper core solenoid coil as found in a #3462/#3472 Milk Car (1949)

Solenoid Coil as found in the #3662/#3672 Milk Cars.

Reverse Unit adaptation as found in the #3359/#3361 Twin Bin Dump Cars.

The "Vibrotor" Motor as found in the #3520 and #3620 Searchlight Cars, as well as the #3535 Security Car.

"String & Spring" vibrating motor as found in the #3435 Aquarium Car.

You may be surprised to see two apparently "motorized" units in this chapter. After all, they do have real "motors" incorporated into them to drive their main operating features.

The first unit, the #3927 Track Cleaning Car has always been considered an "Operating Car" simply because its motor was only used to rotate a round, moistened "sponge" to clean the track. The vehicle itself was not self-propelled. It had to be towed around the track by a locomotive (e.g., a steamer, a diesel, or even one of the motorized switchers in this volume) in order to be used.

The second unit, the #3360 Burro Crane, had an amazing amount of motor-driven functionality built into it. One of those functions was the ability to propel itself along the track under its own power. Over the years, this Crane has come to be viewed as a "Motorized Unit". But the  Lionel Service Manual always classified it as an Operating Car. The Service Manual view was adopted here.

✻ The #3356 Horse Car ✻

The #3356 Coil & Bracket Assembly (3356-24)

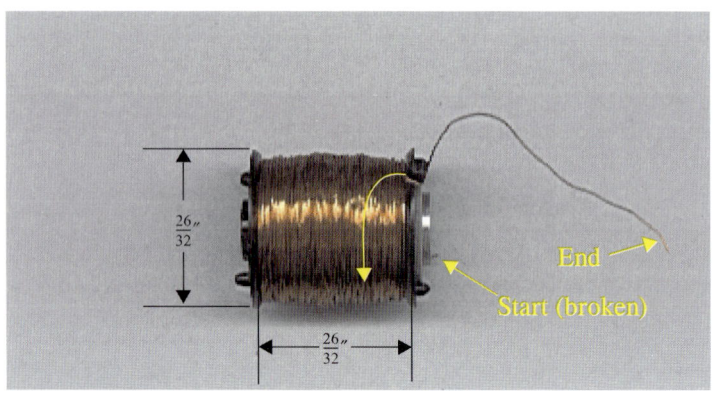

Part Detail	Specifications	
	Wire Size:	29 (0.0110)
	# of Turns:	970
	Style:	Layered ...
	# of Layers:	@18
	Resistance:	11.8 Ω

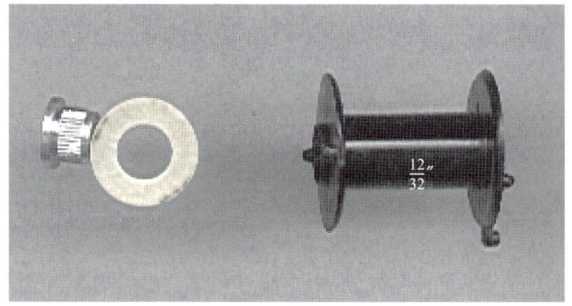

✻ The #3359 Twin Bin Dump Car ✻
✻ The #3361 Lumber Dump Car ✻

The #3359/#3361 Dump Car Coil (3361-16)

Part Detail	Specifications	
	Wire Size:	29 (0.0110)
	# of Turns:	609
	Style:	Layered
	# of Layers:	10
	Resistance :	6.8 Ω

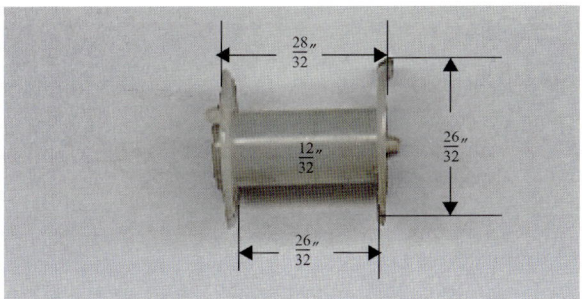

✶ The #3360 Burro Crane Motor ✶

The #3360 Burro Crane Armature (3360-36)

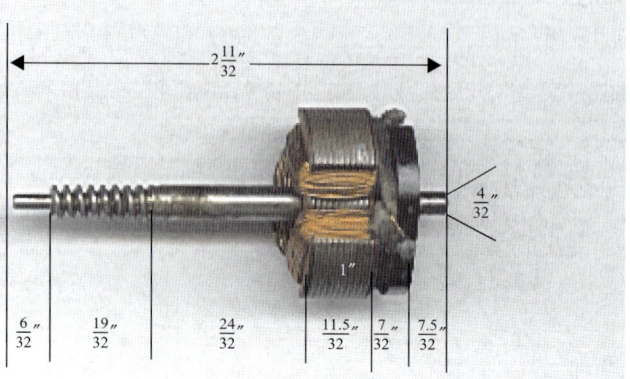

Motor Detail	Specifications	
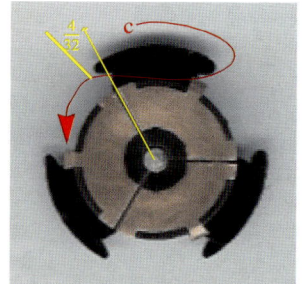	Wire Size:	28 (0.0126)
	# of Turns:	60
	Style:	Layered
	# of Layers:	6
	Direction:	Clockwise
	Resistance :	1.2 - 1.4 Ω
	Tie-Off:	Common

The #3360 Burro Crane Field (3360-44)

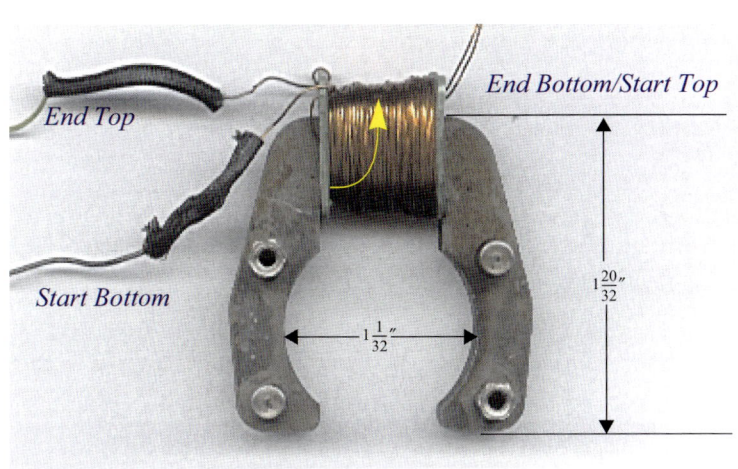

Motor Detail	Specifications	
	Wire Size:	28 (0.0120)
	# of Turns:	Top: 170 Bottom: 175
	Style:	Layered
	# of Layers:	5 (each coil)
	Resistance :	Top: 2.3 Ω Bottom: 2.0 Ω
	Thickness:	10.5/32

✲ The #3366 Corral ✲
✲ The #3366 Circus Car ✲

The #3356 Vibrator Coil (3356-47)

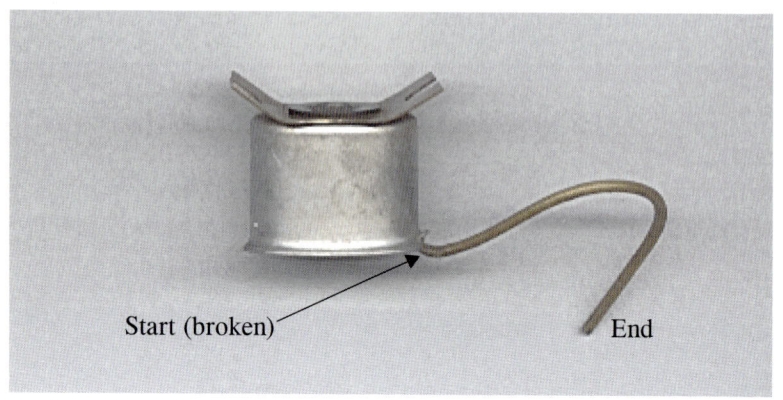

Start (broken)   End

Part Detail	Specifications	
	Wire Size:	29 (0.0107)
	# of Turns:	750
	Style:	Layered ...
	# of Layers:	@14 - 15
	Resistance :	9.6 - 9.7 Ω

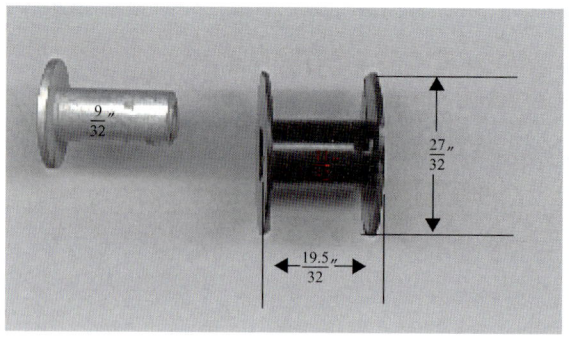

$\frac{9}{32}''$ $\frac{27}{32}''$ $\frac{19.5}{32}''$

O-Gauge - Lionel Postwar Reference Manual

✼ *The #3424 Operating Brakeman Car* ✼
The #3424 Coil Assembly (3424-25)

Part Detail	Specifications	
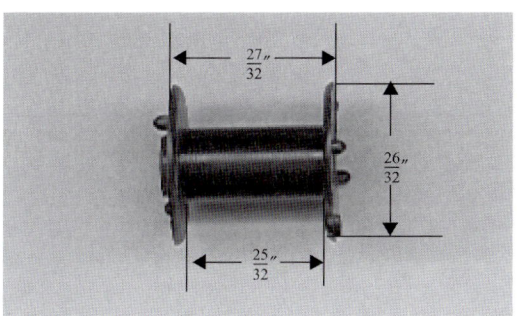	Wire Size:	27 (0.0138)
	# of Turns:	603
	Style:	Layered
	# of Layers:	10
	Resistance :	4.9 Ω

✳ The #3435 Aquarium Car ✳

The #3435 Coil Assembly (3435-7)

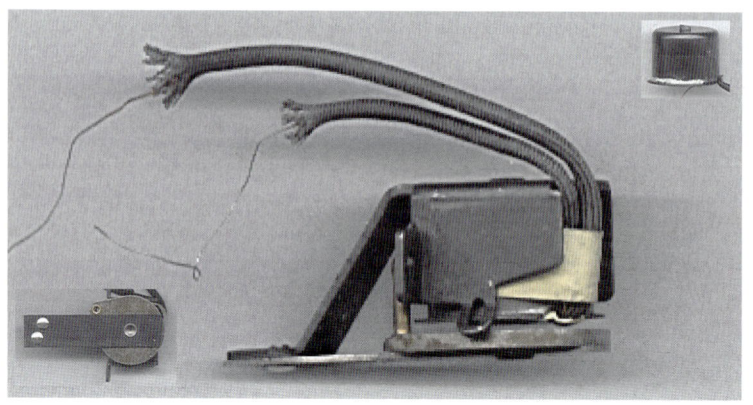

Part Detail	Specifications	
	Wire Size:	29 (0.0110)
	# of Turns:	758
	Style:	Random
	# of Layers:	@18
	Resistance :	9.6 - 9.7 Ω

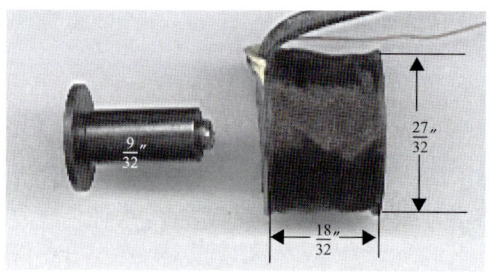

✷ *The #3444 Animated Gondola* ✷

The #3444 Animated Gondola Coil (3444-29)

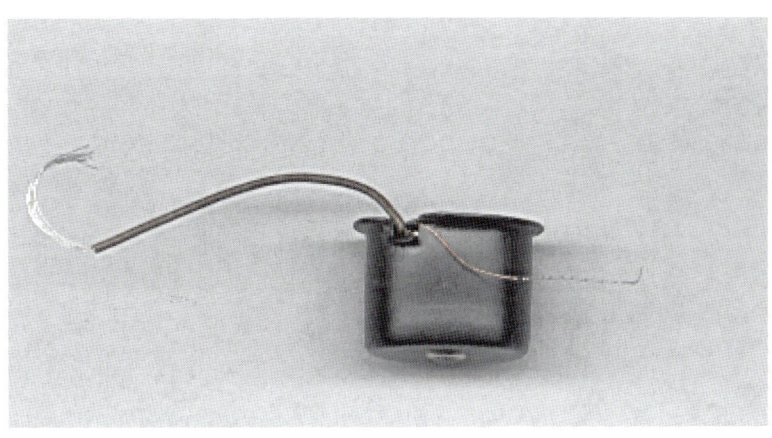

Part Detail	Specifications	
	Wire Size:	29 (0.0108)
	# of Turns:	770
	Style:	Layered ...
	# of Layers:	@17
	Resistance :	9.9 Ω

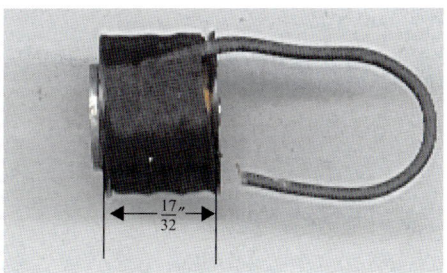

✳ The #3451 Lumber Car ✳
✳ The #3461 Operating Lumber Car ✳

The #3451/#3461 Coil (3451-32)

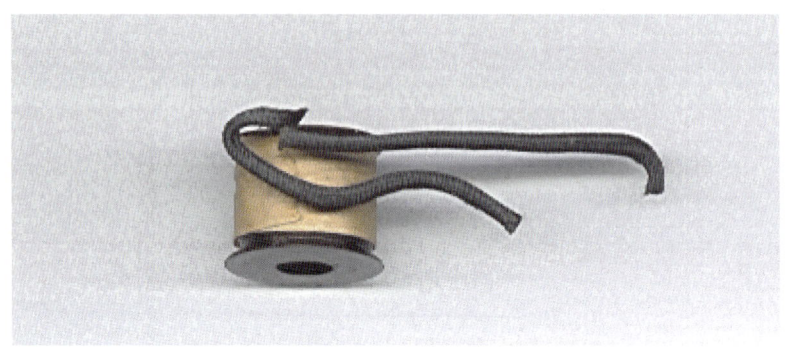

Part Detail	Specifications	
	Wire Size:	26 (0.0153)
	# of Turns:	380
	Style:	Layered
	# of Layers:	12
	Resistance :	2.5 Ω

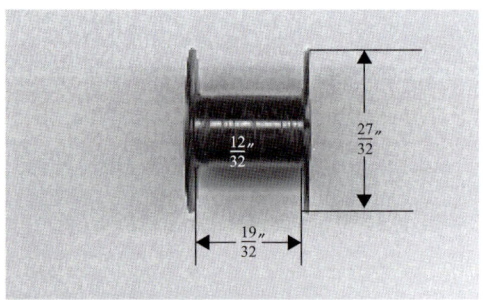

✷ The #3454 Merchandise Car ✷

The #3454 Coil (3454-13)

Part Detail	Specifications	
	Wire Size:	26 (0.0152)
	# of Turns:	401
	Style:	Layered
	# of Layers:	8
	Resistance :	2.3 - 2.4 Ω

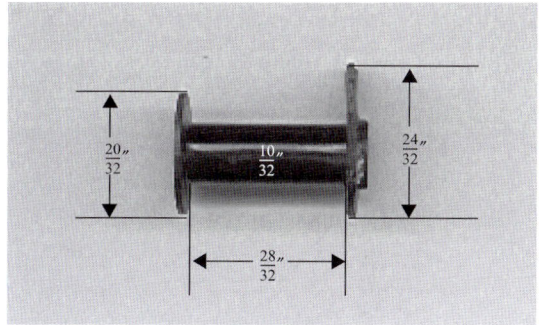

✳ The #3459 Automatic Dump Car ✳
✳ The #3469 Ore Dump Car ✳

The #3459/#3469 Coil (3451-72)

Part Detail	Specifications	
	Wire Size:	26 (0.0155)
	# of Turns:	390
	Style:	Layered
	# of Layers:	12
	Resistance :	2.6 - 2.7 Ω

Note: Figure says 3451-72; Parts list says 3451-32;

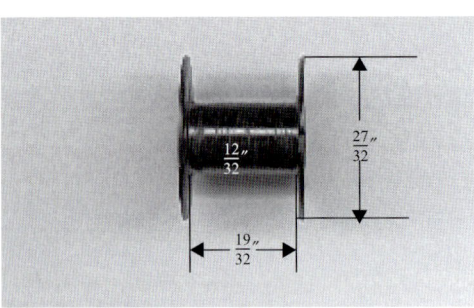

✶ The #3462 Milk Car ✶
✶ The #3472 ('49) Milk Car ✶

The #3462/#3472 ('49) Coil (3462-81)

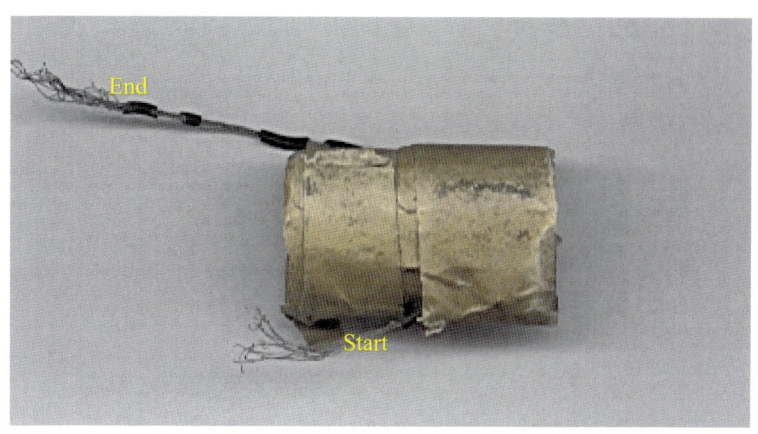

Part Detail	Specifications	
	Wire Size:	22 (0.0248)
	# of Turns:	300
	Style:	Layered
	# of Layers:	7
	Resistance :	1.1 Ω

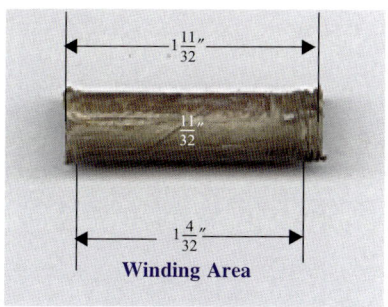

Winding Area

✱ The #3472 Milk Car ✱
The #3472 Coil (3472-37)

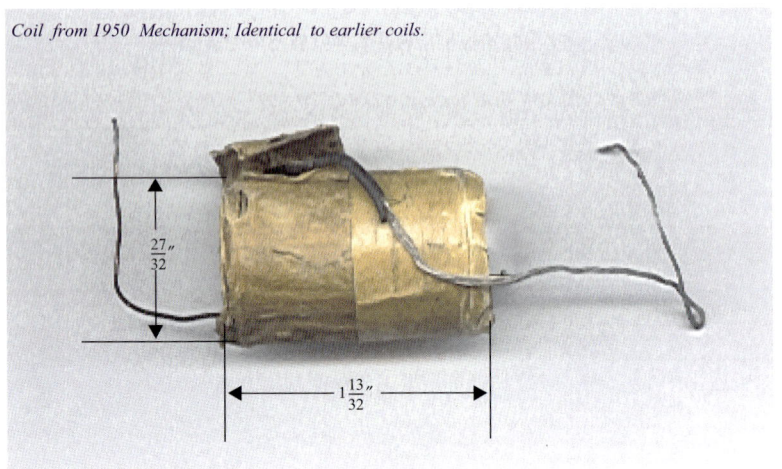

Coil from 1950 Mechanism; Identical to earlier coils.

Part Detail	Specifications	
From '50 Mechanism; 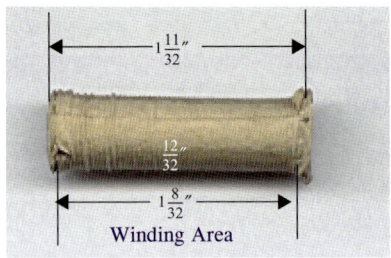	Wire Size:	22 (0.0242
	# of Turns:	330
	Style:	Layered
	# of Layers:	7
	Resistance :	1.2 - 1.3 Ω

4-15 O-Gauge - Lionel POSTWAR REFERENCE Manual

✳ The #3482 Milk Car ✳

The #3482 Coil (3482-14)

Start
End
Bobbin also came in pink nylon

Part Detail	Specifications	
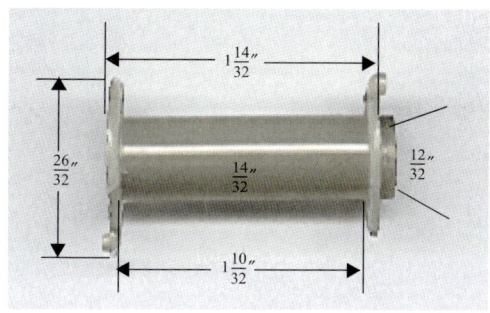	Wire Size:	25 (0.0174)
	# of Turns:	375
	Style:	Layered ...
	# of Layers:	6
	Resistance :	2.2 - 2.2 Ω

✤ *The #3520 Searchlight Coil* ✤
✤ *The #3620 Searchlight Coil* ✤

The #3520/#3620 Searchlight Coil (3520-20)

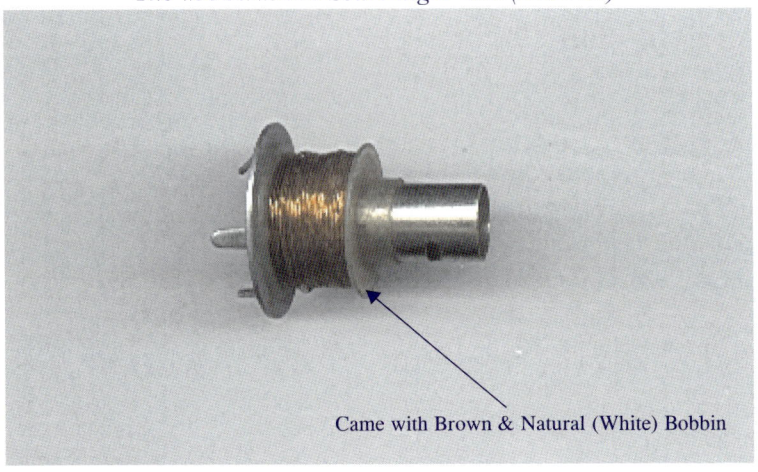

Came with Brown & Natural (White) Bobbin

(Cf. #494 Rotary Beacon Coil)

Part Detail	Specifications	
	Wire Size:	31 (0.0083)
	# of Turns:	833
	Style:	Layered ...
	# of Layers:	20
	Resistance :	14.2 Ω

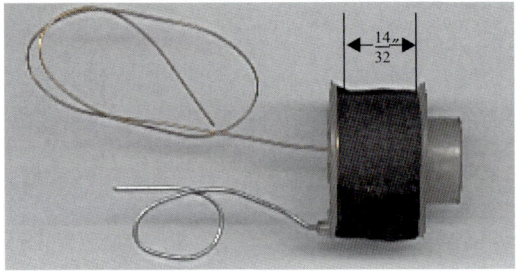

The #3530 Generator Car

The #3530 Coil& Bracket (3530-46)

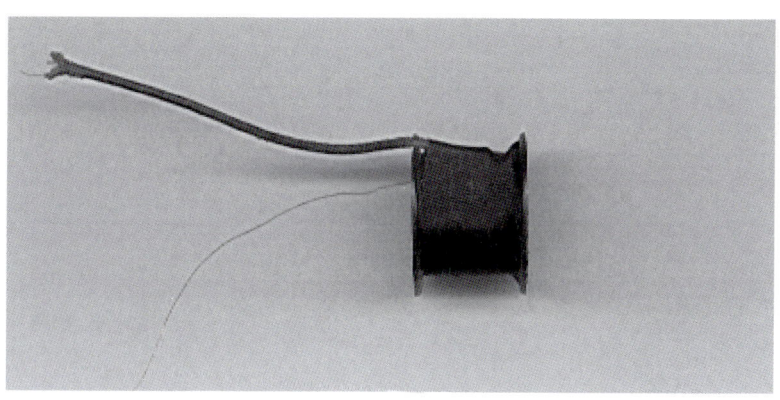

Part Detail	Specifications	
	Wire Size:	36 (0.0048)
	# of Turns:	2152
	Style:	Random
	# of Layers:	Indeterminate
	Resistance :	117.0 Ω

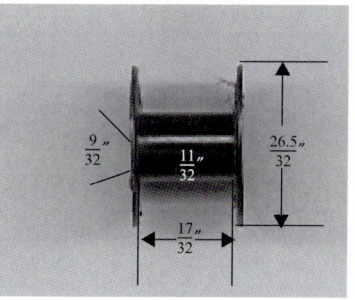

✸ The #3535 Security Car ✸

The #3535 Coil, Socket & Plate (3535-7)

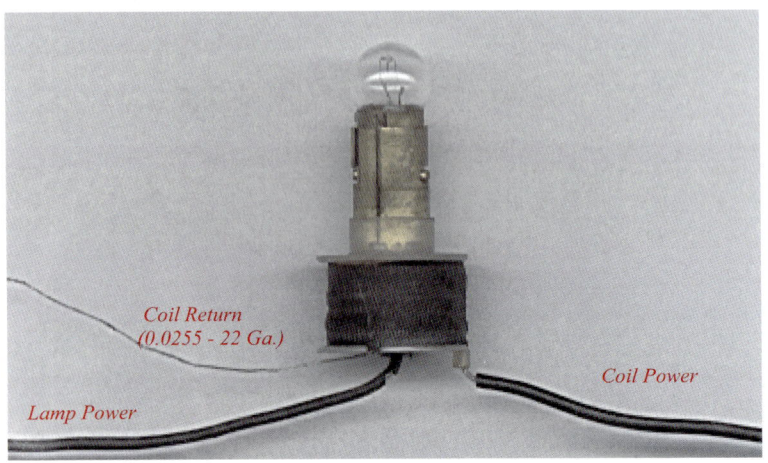

Coil Return (0.0255 - 22 Ga.)

Lamp Power

Coil Power

Lamp Return is via rivet when secured to frame.

Part Detail	Specifications	
	Wire Size:	31 (0.0083 - 0.0085)
	# of Turns:	808 - 833
	Style:	Layered ...
	# of Layers:	20
	Resistance :	14.2 - 14.4 Ω

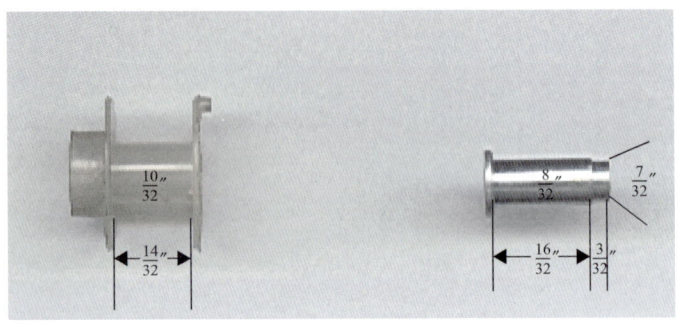

✳ The #3559 Dump Car ✳

The #3559 Dump Car (3859-5)

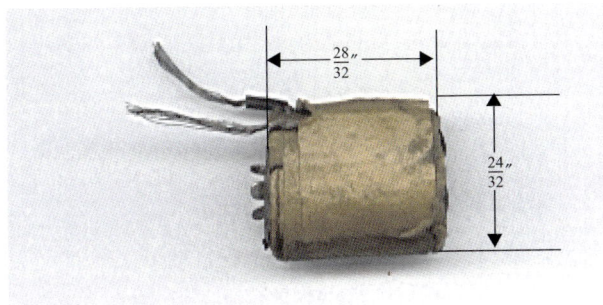

Part Detail	Specifications	
	Wire Size:	26 (0.0154)
	# of Turns:	418
	Style:	Layered
	# of Layers:	10
	Resistance:	2.7 - 2.8 Ω

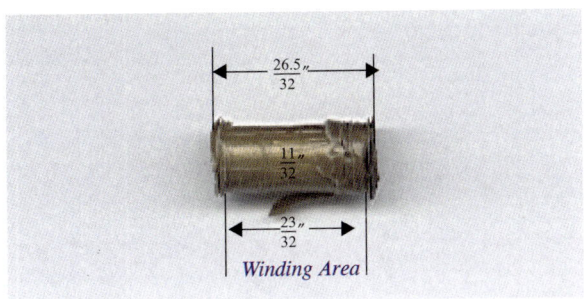

✻ The #3562 Operating Barrel Car ✻

The #3562 Coil Assembly (362-22)

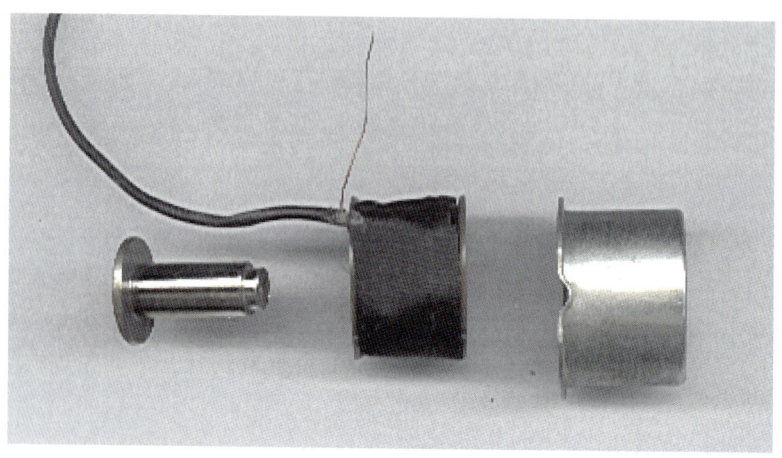

Part Detail	Specifications	
	Wire Size:	29 (0.0109)
	# of Turns:	751
	Style:	Layered
	# of Layers:	18
	Resistance :	9.4 - 9.5 Ω

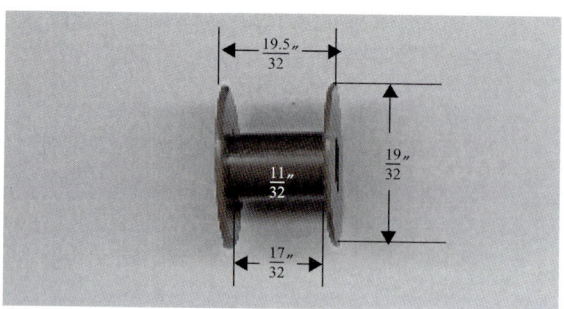

✳ *The #3656 Stock Car & Platform* ✳

The #3656 Stock Car Coil Assembly   (3656-28)

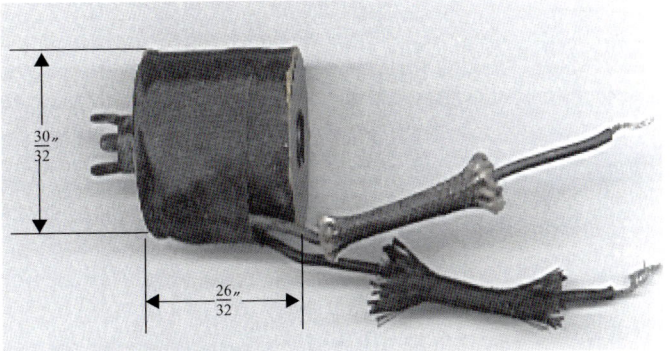

Part Detail	Specifications	
	Wire Size:	29 (0.0108)
	# of Turns:	1052
	Style:	Layered
	# of Layers:	20
	Resistance :	14.8 - 14.9 Ω

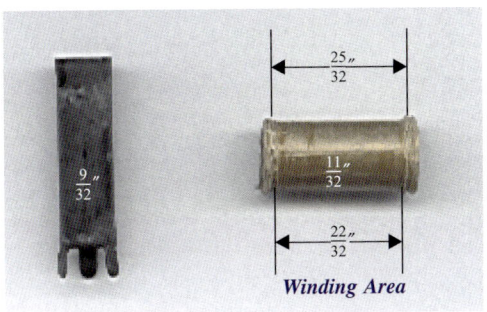

Winding Area

The #3656 Platform Coil Assembly ('49) (3656-138)

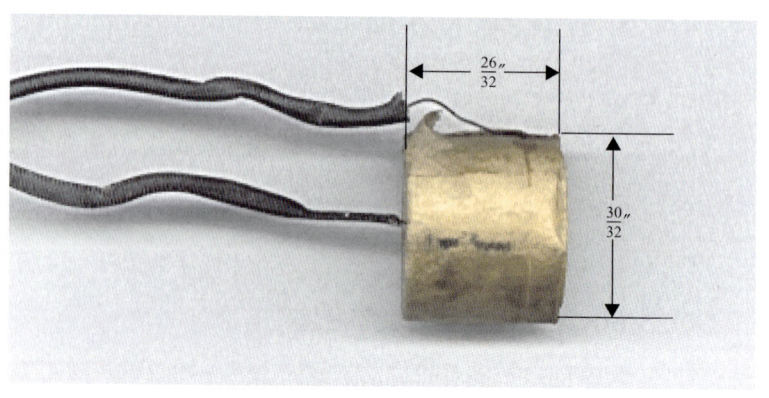

Part Detail	Specifications	
	Wire Size:	27 (0.0138)
	# of Turns:	688
	Style:	Layered
	# of Layers:	17
	Resistance:	6.5 Ω

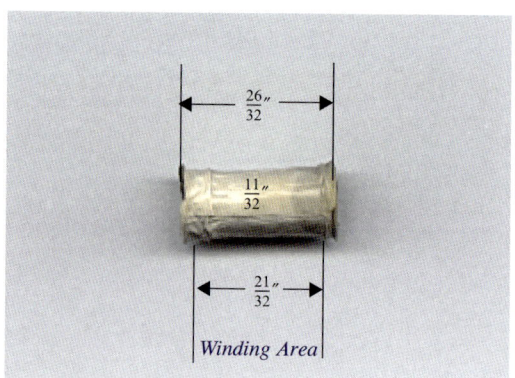

The #3656 Platform Coil Assembly ('50-'54) (3656-189)
Note: Service Manual also lists as: 3656-185

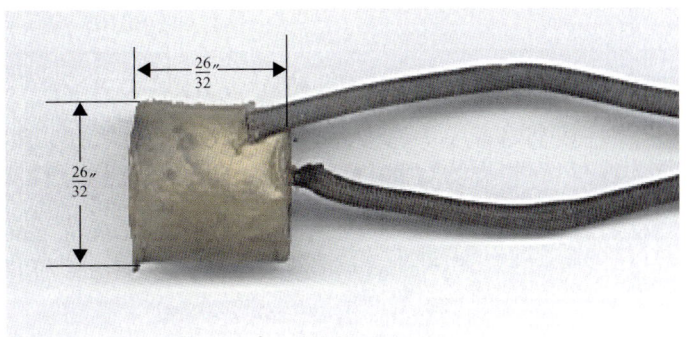

Part Detail	Specifications	
	Wire Size:	30 (0.0100)
	# of Turns:	783
	Style:	Layered
	# of Layers:	16
	Resistance :	10.2 - 10.3 Ω

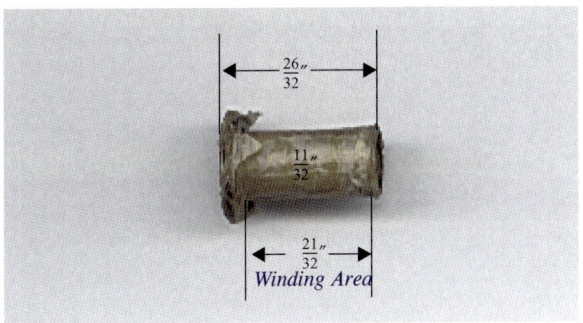

* *The #3662 Milk Car* *
* *The #3672 Bosco Milk Car* *

The #3662/#3672 Milk Car Coil (3662-66)

Part Detail	Specifications	
	Wire Size:	24 (0.0195)
	# of Turns:	448
	Style:	Layered
	# of Layers:	8
	Resistance :	2.1 - 2.2 Ω

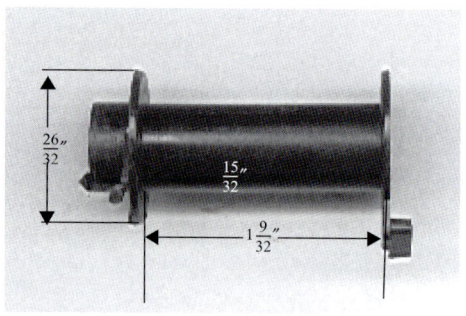

O-Gauge - Lionel POSTWAR REFERENCE Manual

✻ *The #3927 Track Cleaning Car* ✻

The #3927 Track Cleaning Car Armature (3927-11)

Note: Not Self-Propelled. Motor operates rotary track cleaner.

Motor Detail	Specifications	
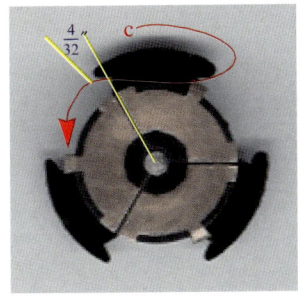	Wire Size:	27 (0.0130)
	# of Turns:	57
	Style:	Layered
	# of Layers:	6
	Direction:	Clockwise
	Resistance :	1.1 - 1.2 Ω
	Tie-Off:	Common

The #3927 Track Clean Car Field (41-28)

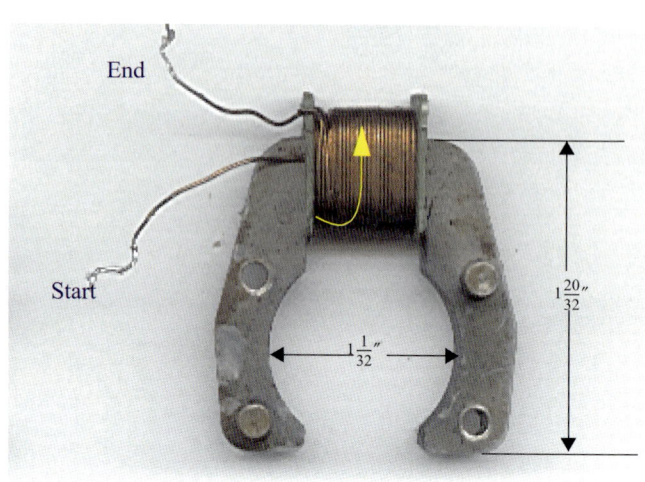

Motor Detail	Specifications	
	Wire Size:	24 (0.0195)
	# of Turns:	132
	Style:	Layered
	# of Layers:	6
	Resistance:	.9 - 1.0 Ω
	Thickness:	11/32"

CHAPTER 5 *Accessories*

In this chapter, you will find the components that "gave life" to one of the most interesting lines of accessories in the world of toy trains. The "motor" technology is especially interesting when viewed in terms of the totally arbitrary evolution described below.

Technology reminiscent of the pre-war Lionel Jr. motor, the coal loader and Bascule bridge motors were built up from stamped steel side-frames and spacers. Another carryover, the OO-Gauge motor previously used in the #165 Crane, was used in the immediate postwar #182 Magnetic Crane and #38 Water Tower.

The next leap: Adaptation (reengineering) of the then current O-Gauge Locomotive motor technology; heavy cast-metal housing containing an intricate gear and bearing system. Very large form-factor requiring a large amount of real-estate, but very powerful.

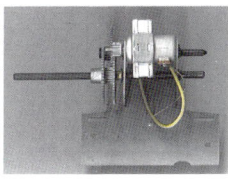

A brief flirtation with a form of the "can" motor. No brushes; just plain copper strips in direct contact with the commutator.

Development of the "Vibrotor" or "String and Spring" Motor. Not the most powerful motor, but adequate to generate motion using a system of pulleys and reduction gears. Freed up a lot of real-estate resulting in more realistic looking operating accessories.

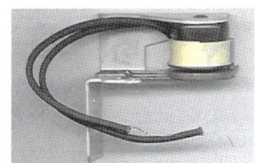

✻ The #30 Water Tower ✻
✻ The #38 Water Tower ✻

The #30/#38 Water Tower Spout Coil (3652-30)

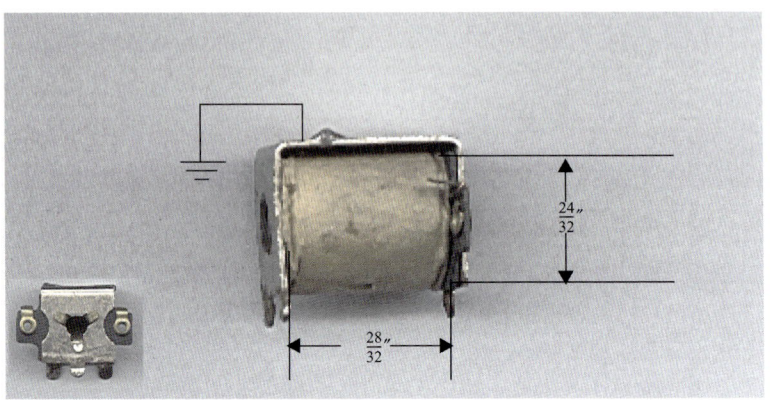

(Note: Mounting Plate & Coil Assembly is 38-12)

Part Detail	Specifications	
	Wire Size:	26 (0.0155)
	# of Turns:	432
	Style:	Layered
	# of Layers:	10
	Resistance :	2.8 - 2.9 Ω

The #38 Water Tower Pump Armature (38P-11)

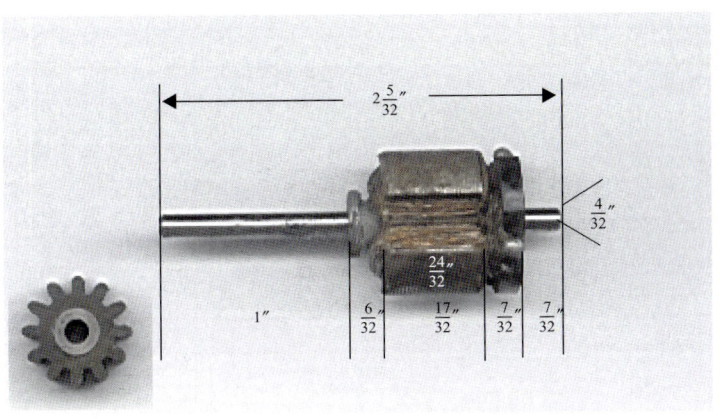

Motor Detail	Specifications	
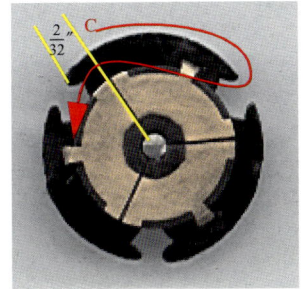	Wire Size:	30 (0.0093)
	# of Turns:	71 - 72
	Style:	Layered
	# of Layers:	8
	Direction:	Clockwise
	Resistance:	2.3 - 2.4 Ω
	Tie-Off:	Common

The #38 Water Tower Pump Field

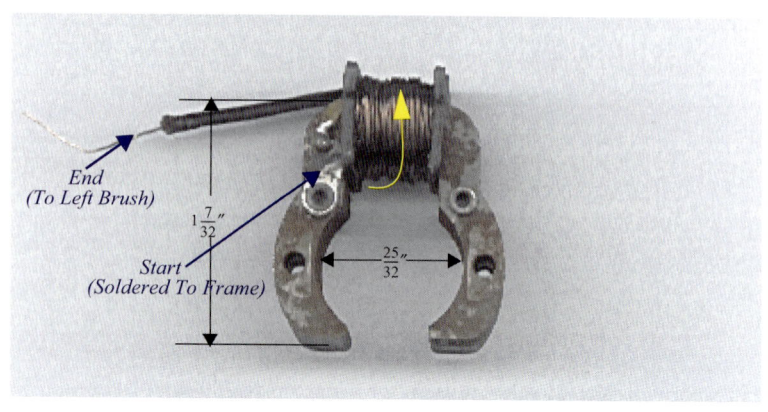

End (To Left Brush)

Start (Soldered To Frame)

$1\frac{7}{32}''$

$\frac{25}{32}''$

Motor Detail	Specifications	
	Wire Size:	27 (0.0135)
	# of Turns:	165
	Style:	Layered
	# of Layers:	6
	Resistance:	1.6 - 1.7 Ω
	Thickness:	16/32"

✻ The #45 Gateman ✻
✻ The #45N Automatic Gateman ✻

The #45/#45N Gateman Coil (138-18)

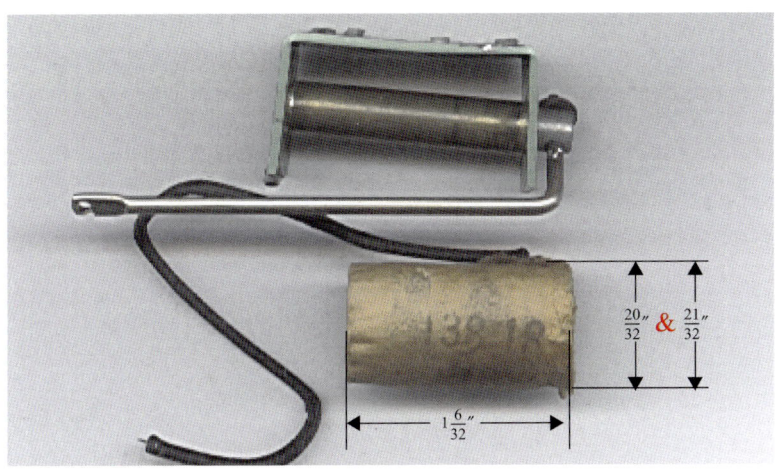

(Note: 2 Different Core Sizes Noted = 2 Different Ω Values)

Part Detail	Specifications	
	Wire Size:	28 (0.0120)
	# of Turns:	655
	Style:	Layered
	# of Layers:	10
	Resistance : 10/32" Cores: 11/32" Cores	 5.7 - 5.8 Ω 6.5 - 6.6 Ω

Winding Area

O-Gauge - Lionel Postwar Reference Manual   5-5

✻ The #97 Coal Elevator ✻
✻ The #164 Lumber Loader ✻

The #97/#164 Motor Armature (97M-6)

Motor Detail	Specifications	
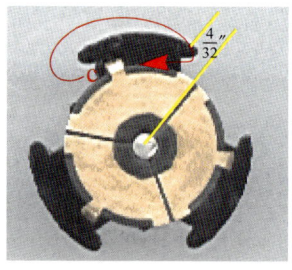	Wire Size:	27 (0.0140)
	# of Turns:	57-62
	Style:	Layered
	# of Layers:	6
	Direction:	Clockwise
	Resistance :	1.0 - 1.1 Ω
	Tie-Off:	Common

The #97/#164 Motor Field

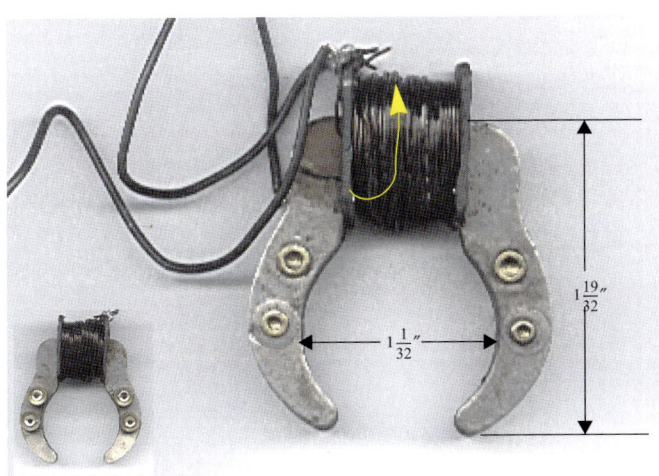

Motor Detail	Specifications	
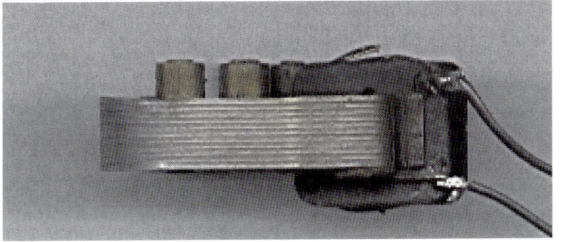	Wire Size:	24 (0.0195)
	# of Turns:	188
	Style:	Layered
	# of Layers:	8
	Resistance :	1.1 - 1.2 Ω
	Thickness:	12/32"

The #97 Coal Elevator Scoop Coil (97-9)

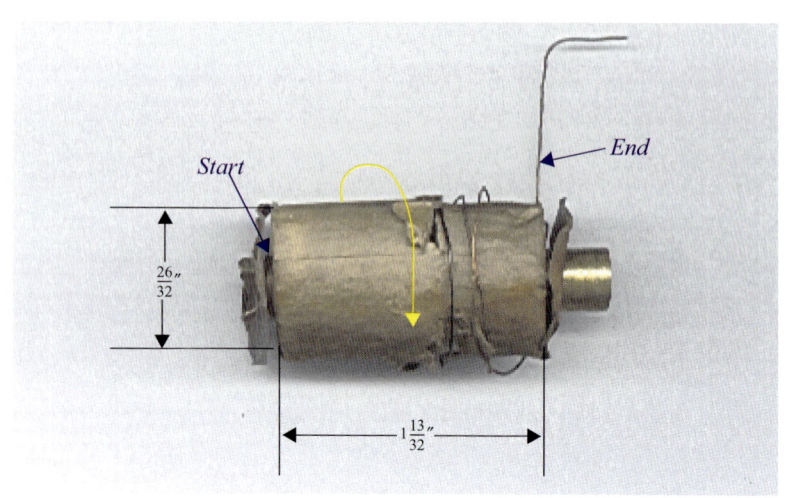

Part Detail	Specifications	
	Wire Size:	26 (0.0152)
	# of Turns:	665
	Style:	Layered
	# of Layers:	10.5
	Resistance :	4.5 - 4.7 Ω

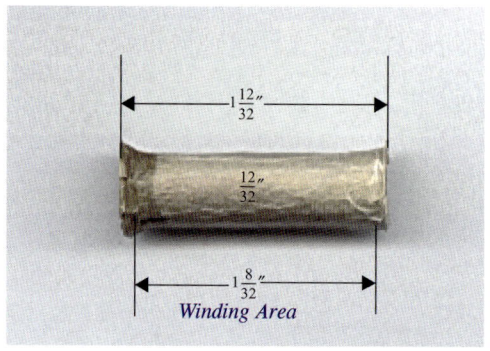

The #97 Coal Elevator Chute Coil (97-21)

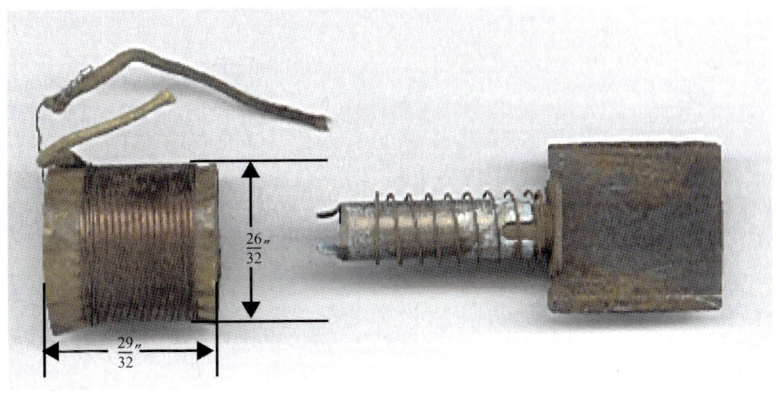

Part Detail	Specifications	
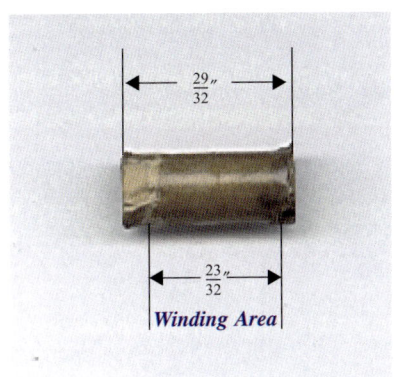	Wire Size:	28 (0.0123)
	# of Turns:	690
	Style:	Layered
	# of Layers:	14
	Resistance :	7.2 - 7.4 Ω

Winding Area

The #164 Lumber Loader Coil & Bracket Assembly (164-13)

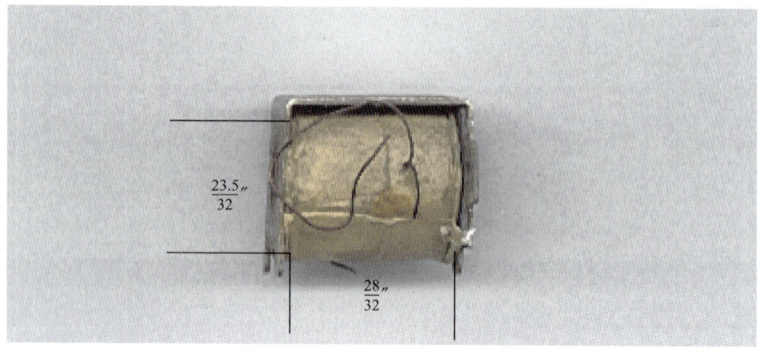

(Note: Coil alone is the 3652-30 and is also used in the #30 & #38.)

Part Detail	Specifications	
	Wire Size:	26 (0.0155)
	# of Turns:	440
	Style:	Layered
	# of Layers:	9.5
	Resistance:	2.8 - 3.0 Ω

Winding Area

✻ The #128 Animated Newsstand ✻

The 128 Animated Newsstand Motor (128-15)

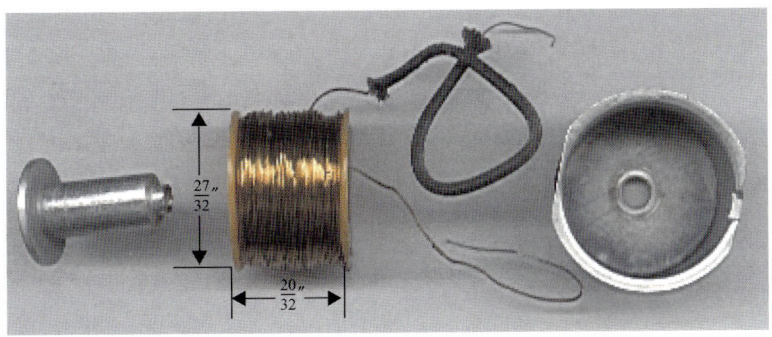

Part Detail	Specifications	
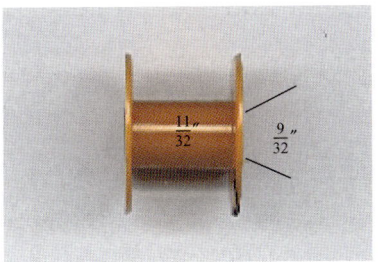	Wire Size:	29 (0.0110)
	# of Turns:	750
	Style:	Random
	# of Layers:	Indeterminate
	Resistance :	9.4 - 9.5 Ω

✽ *The #138 Water Tower* ✽

The 138 Water Tower Coil (138-23)

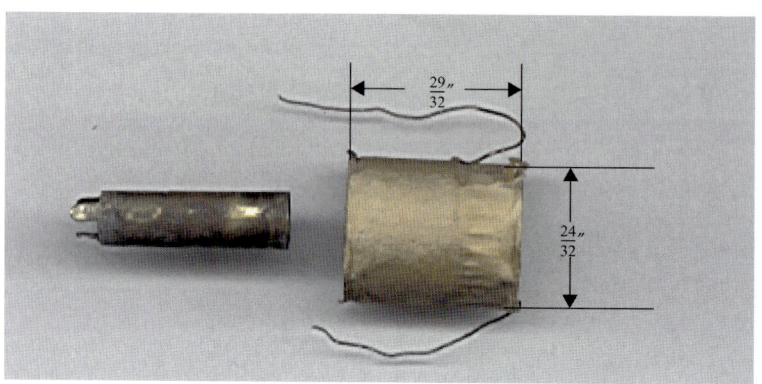

Part Detail	Specifications	
	Wire Size:	26 (0.0155)
	# of Turns:	443
	Style:	Layered
	# of Layers:	9.75
	Resistance :	2.8 - 2.9 Ω

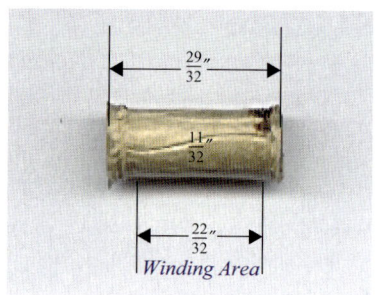

✳ *The #140 Banjo Signal* ✳

The #140 Banjo Signal Coil (140-19)

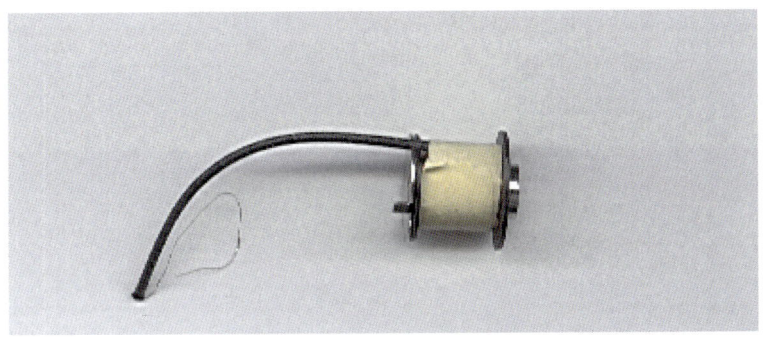

Part Detail	Specifications	
	Wire Size:	38 (0.0041)
	# of Turns:	1910
	Style:	Random
	# of Layers:	Indeterminate
	Resistance :	78.5 - 87.3 Ω

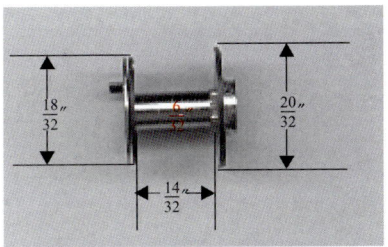

✱ The #145 Automatic Gateman ✱
✱ The #1047 Switchman ✱

The #145/#1047 Coil (145-5)

Part Detail	Specifications	
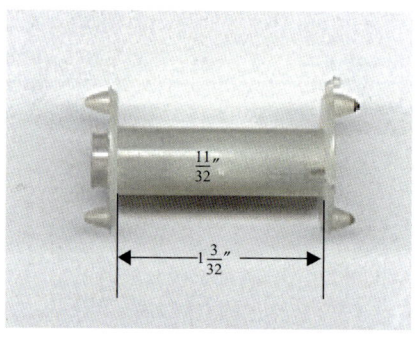	Wire Size:	27 (0.0140)
	# of Turns:	800
	Style:	Layered ...
	# of Layers:	@12
	Resistance :	5.7 - 5.8 Ω

✱ The #151 Semaphore ('51) ✱

The 151 Semaphore Coil (151-55)

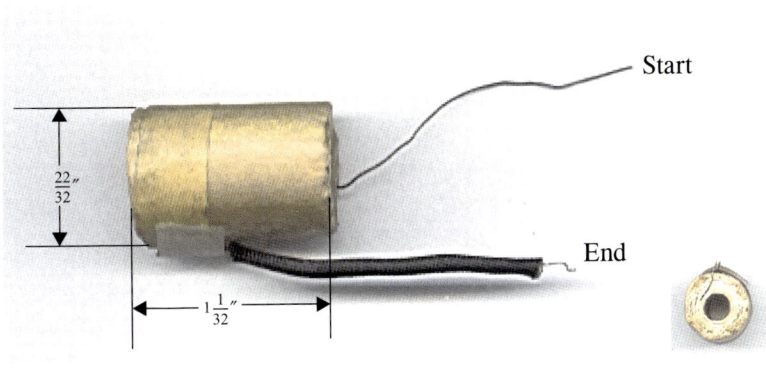

Part Detail	Specifications	
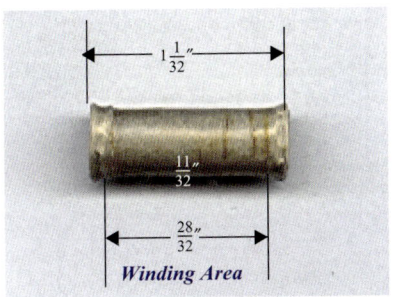	Wire Size:	28 (0.0120)
	# of Turns:	627
	Style:	Layered
	# of Layers:	11
	Resistance :	5.8 - 6.0 Ω

✳ The #151 Semaphore ('54/'59) ✳

The 151 Semaphore Coil (711-127)

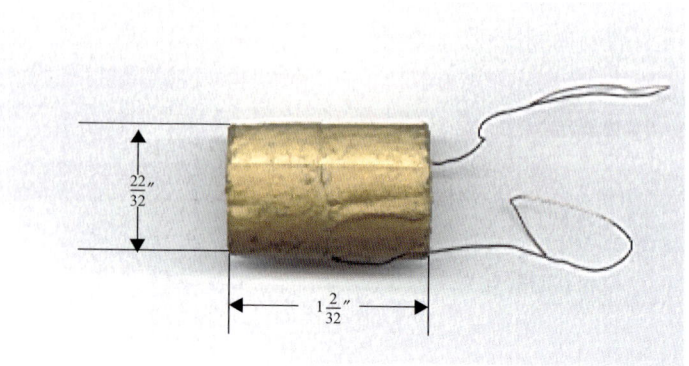

(Note: Same coil used in O22 Track Switch)

Part Detail	Specifications	
	Wire Size:	29 (0.0104)
	# of Turns:	720
	Style:	Layered
	# of Layers:	11.5
	Resistance:	8.0 - 8.2 Ω

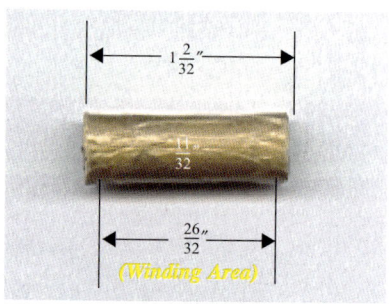

(Winding Area)

✻ *The #152 Crossing Gate* ✻

The 152 Crossing Gate Coil (152-4)

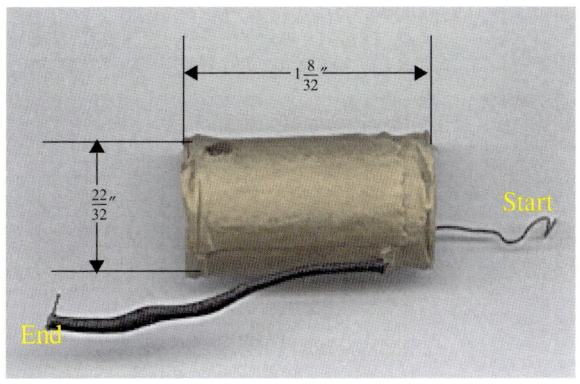

Part Detail	Specifications	
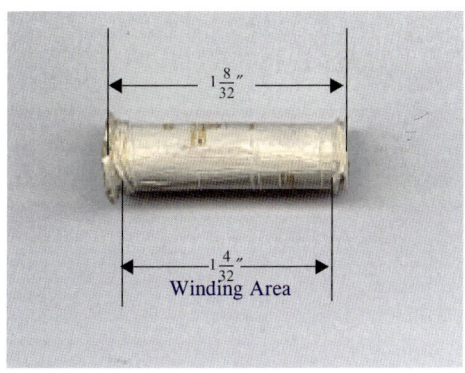	Wire Size:	27 (0.0136)
	# of Turns:	714
	Style:	Layered
	# of Layers:	10
	Resistance :	5.3 - 5.4 Ω

The #155 Ringing Signal *

The 155 Ringing Signal Coil (155-10)

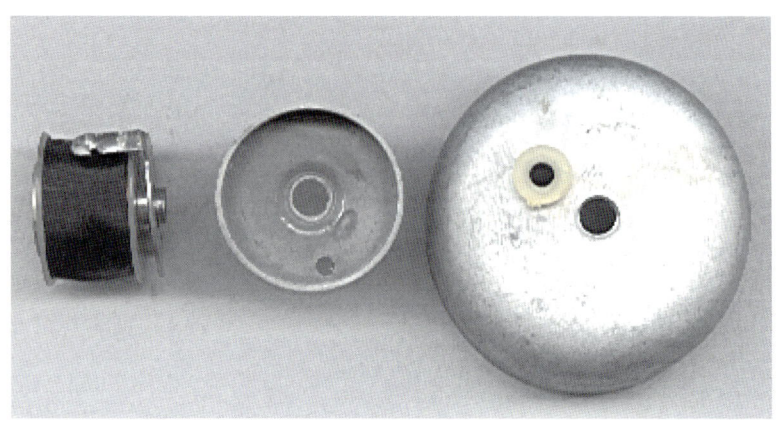

Part Detail	Specifications	
	Wire Size:	33 (0.0069)
	# of Turns:	1210
	Style:	Random
	# of Layers:	Indeterminate
	Resistance :	32.2 - 32.4 Ω

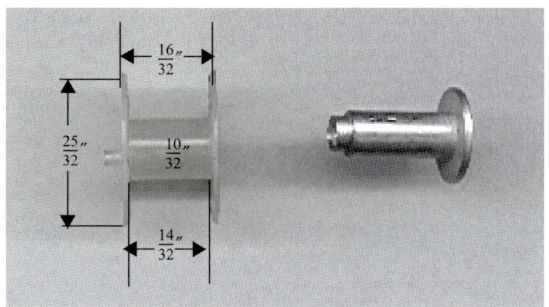

✳ The #161 Mailbag Pickup ✳

The 161 Mailbag Pickup (161-11)

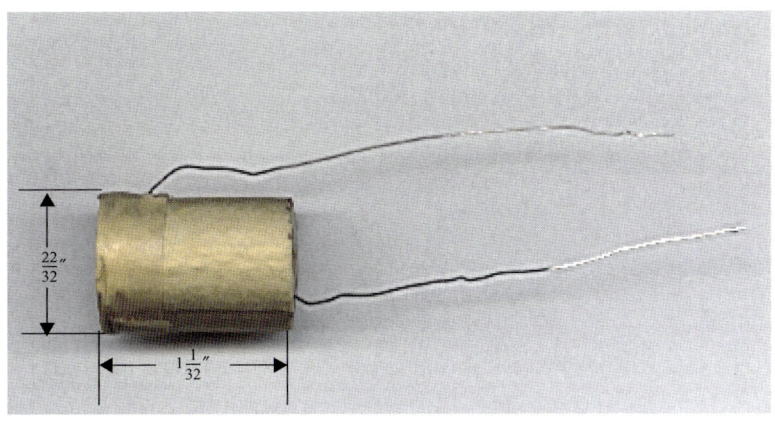

Part Detail	Specifications	
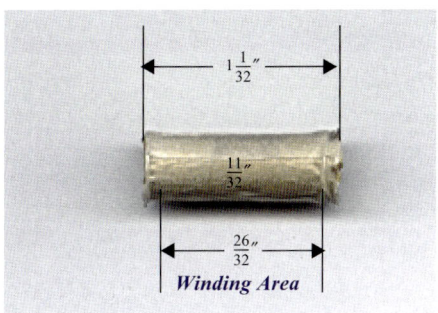	Wire Size:	28 (0.0123)
	# of Turns:	623
	Style:	Layered
	# of Layers:	11
	Resistance :	5.7 - 5.9 Ω

O-Gauge - Lionel Postwar Reference Manual

✱ *The #182 Remote Magnet Crane* ✱

The #182 Motor Armature (165M-8)

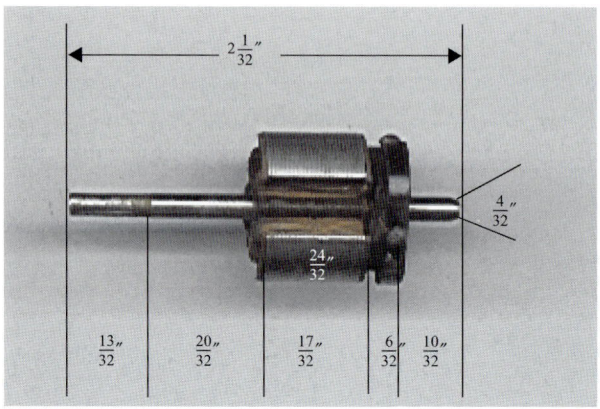

Motor Detail	Specifications	
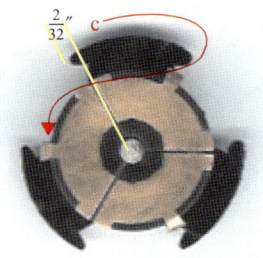	Wire Size:	30 (0.0095)
	# of Turns:	56
	Style:	Layered
	# of Layers:	6
	Direction:	Clockwise
	Resistance :	1.7 - 1.8 Ω
	Tie-Off:	Common

The #182 Motor Field

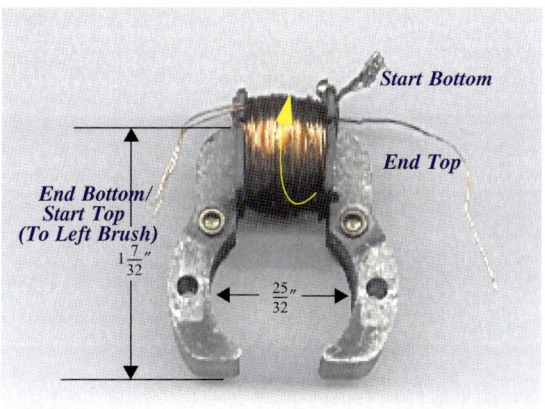

Motor Detail	Specifications	
	Wire Size:	29 (0.0111)
	# of Turns:	Top: 144 - 151
		Bottom: 148 - 155
	Style:	Layered
	# of Layers:	5 (ea. coil)
	Resistance :	Top: 2.3 - 2.4 Ω
		Bottom: 2.1 - 2.2 Ω
	Thickness:	15/32" - 17/32"

Double-Wound Field

The #182 Crane Magnet (182-29)

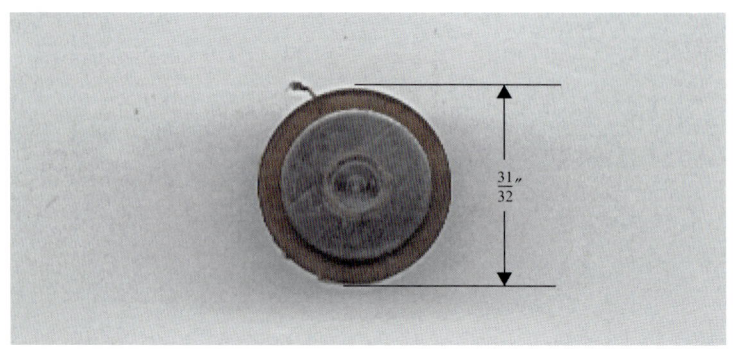

Part Detail	Specifications	
	Wire Size:	31 (0.0085)
	# of Turns:	900
	Style:	Random
	# of Layers:	@28
	Resistance :	18.9 - 19.3 Ω

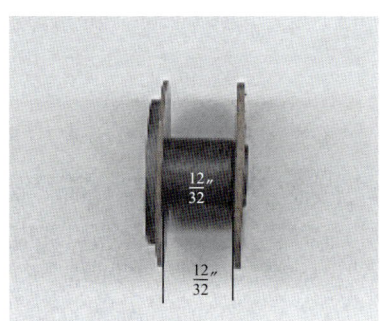

The #182 Crane Coil & Bracket Assy (165-39)

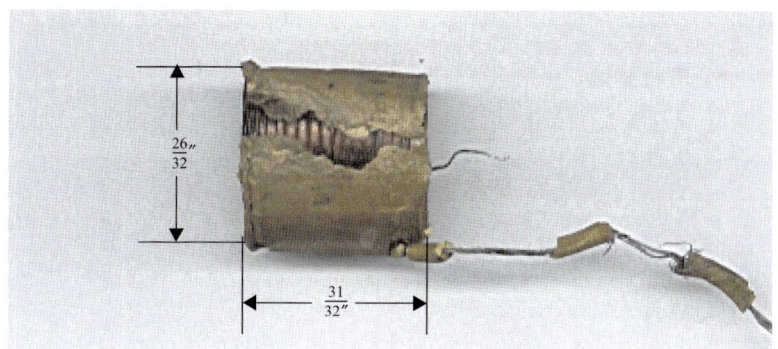

(Note: Start of each coil is grounded to frame).

Part Detail	*Specifications*	
	Wire Size:	29 (0.0110)
	# of Turns:	1055
	Style:	Layered
	# of Layers:	16.25
	Resistance :	13.7 Ω

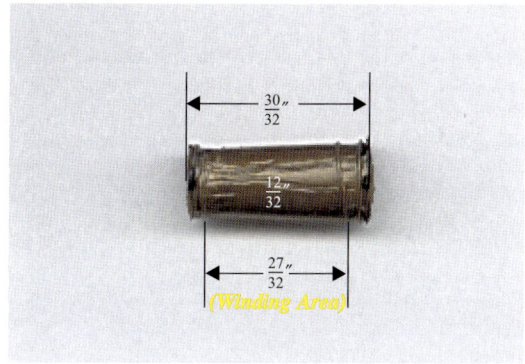

✶ *The #175 Rocket Launcher* ✶

The 175 Rocket Launcher Motor Coil (175-100)

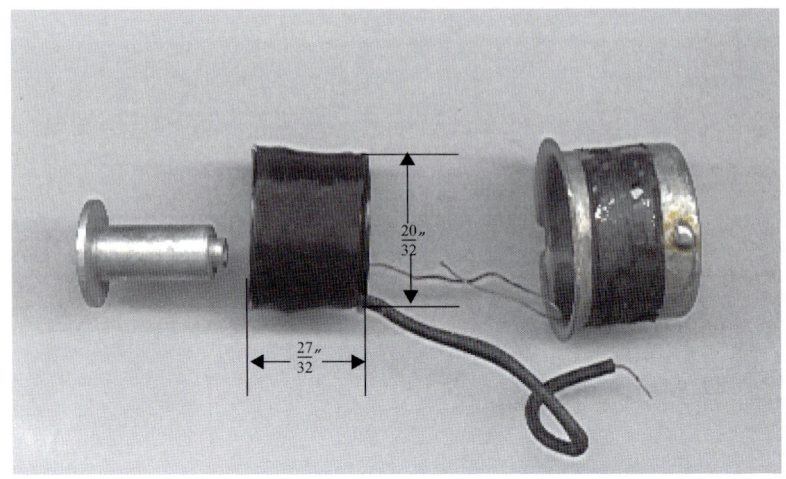

Part Detail	Specifications	
	Wire Size:	29 (0.0110)
	# of Turns:	767
	Style:	Layered
	# of Layers:	18
	Resistance :	9.0 - 9.1 Ω

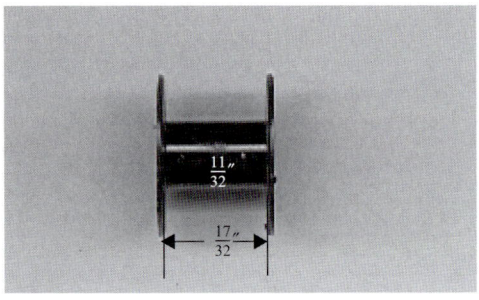

The 175 Rocket Launcher Trigger Coil (175-8)

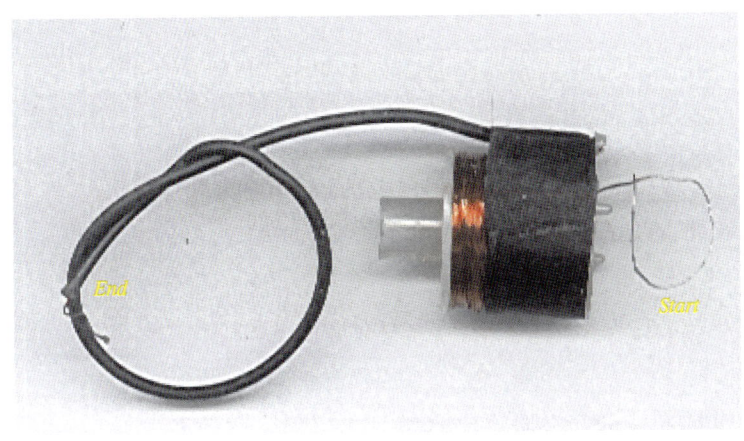

Part Detail	Specifications	
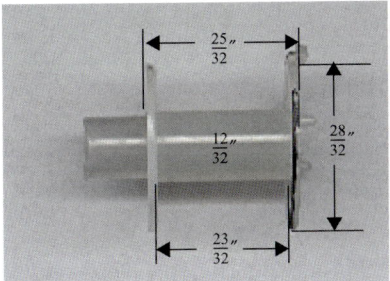	Wire Size:	29 (0.0110)
	# of Turns:	1030
	Style:	Layered ...
	# of Layers:	@20
	Resistance:	13.0 - 13.1 Ω

✳ The #192 Control Tower ✳

The 192 Control Tower Motor (192-31)

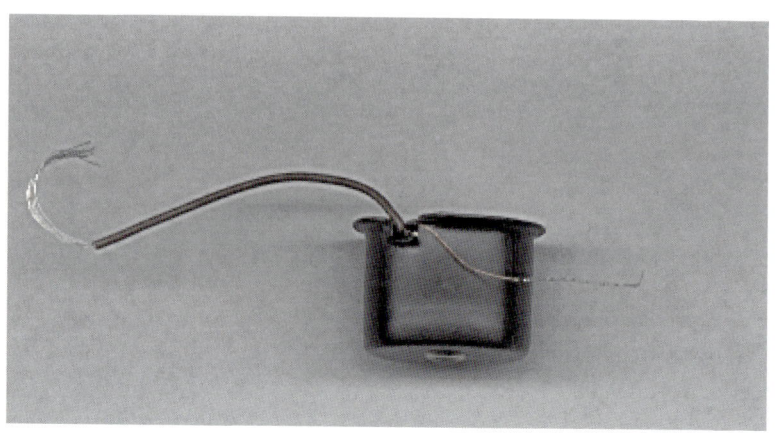

Part Detail	Specifications	
	Wire Size:	32 (0.0077-0.0079)
	# of Turns:	1355
	Style:	Random
	# of Layers:	Indeterminate
	Resistance :	32.3 - 34.7 Ω

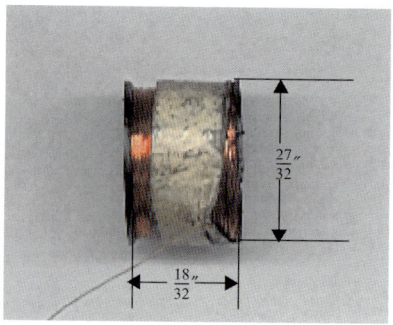

✷ *The #197 Radar Tower* ✷

The 197 Radar Tower Motor (197-26)

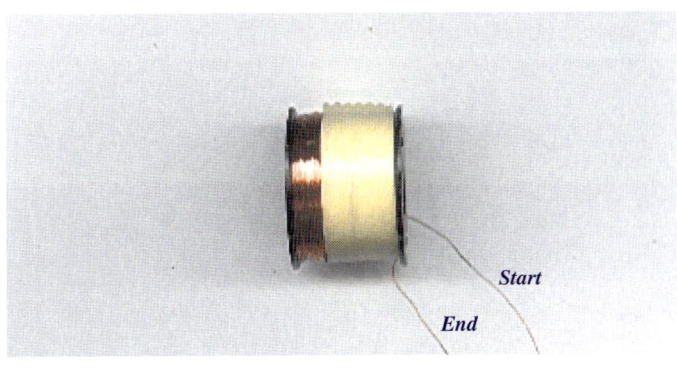

Part Detail	Specifications	
	Wire Size:	32 (0.0077)
	# of Turns:	1386
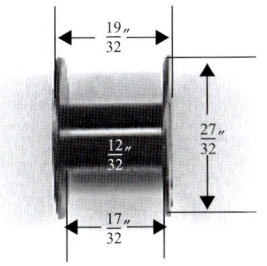	Style:	Random
	# of Layers:	Indeterminate
	Resistance :	32.8 - 32.9 Ω

✻ The #252 Crossing Gate ✻

The 252 Crossing Gate Coil (252-52)

Part Detail	Specifications	
	Wire Size:	30 (0.0095)
	# of Turns:	950
	Style:	Layered ...
	# of Layers:	@10
	Resistance :	11.7 - 11.8 Ω

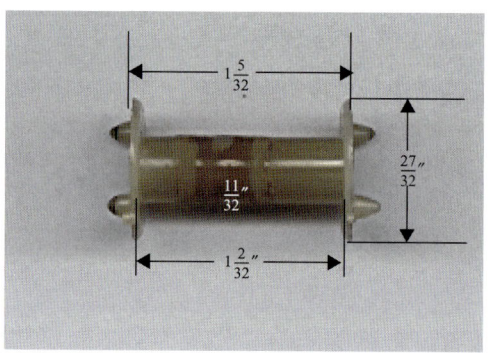

✸ *The #262 Automatic Highway Crossing Signal* ✸

The 262 Highway Signal Coil (262-64)

Part Detail	Specifications	
	Wire Size:	29 (0.0109)
	# of Turns:	1027
	Style:	Layered
	# of Layers:	12
	Resistance :	10.4 - 10.5 Ω

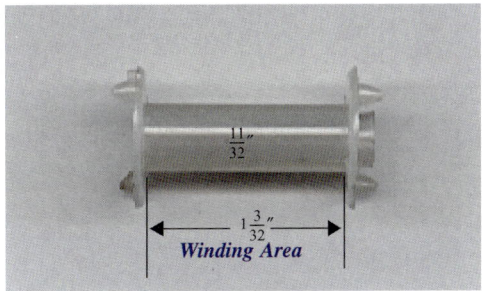

✻ The #264 Lumber Unloader ✻

The 264 Lumber Unloader Motor (264-101)

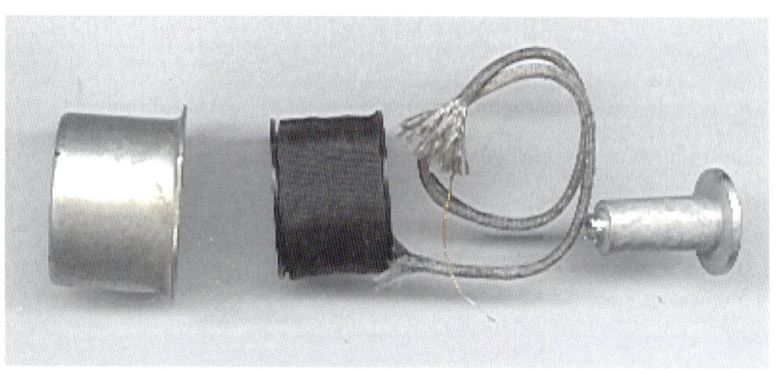

Part Detail	Specifications	
	Wire Size:	29 (0.0110)
	# of Turns:	756
	Style:	Random
	# of Layers:	@18
	Resistance :	9.4 - 9.5 Ω

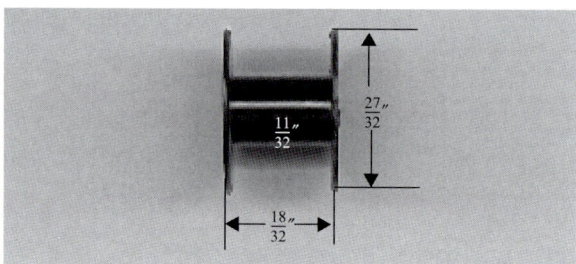

✻ *The #282 Portal Gantry Crane* ✻
✻ *The #282R Gantry Crane* ✻

As documented in available literature, the motor armature and field were basically the same across both units, with the major difference being the mounting bracket. The field is double-wound in both units. The "clutch solenoid" was also changed.

#282 Portal Gantry Crane Motor

#282 Gantry Crane Model R

The #282/#282R Armature (282-106)

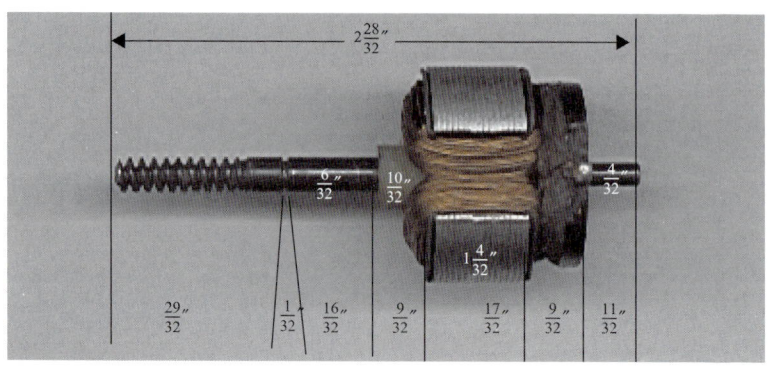

Motor Detail	Specifications	
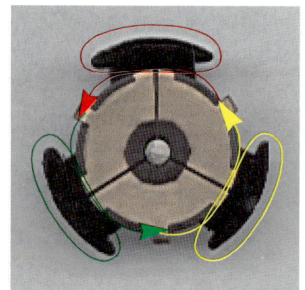 #282 Motor	Wire Size:	28
	# of Turns:	130
	Style:	Layered
	# of Layers:	10
	Direction:	Clockwise
	Resistance :	1.3 - 1.4 Ω
	Tie-Off:	End-To-End

The #282/#282R Motor Field

End Top
Start Bottom
End Bottom/Start Top (Twisted Together)

$1\frac{5}{32}"$

Note: Shown with Broken Bottom Start Lead

Motor Detail	Specifications	
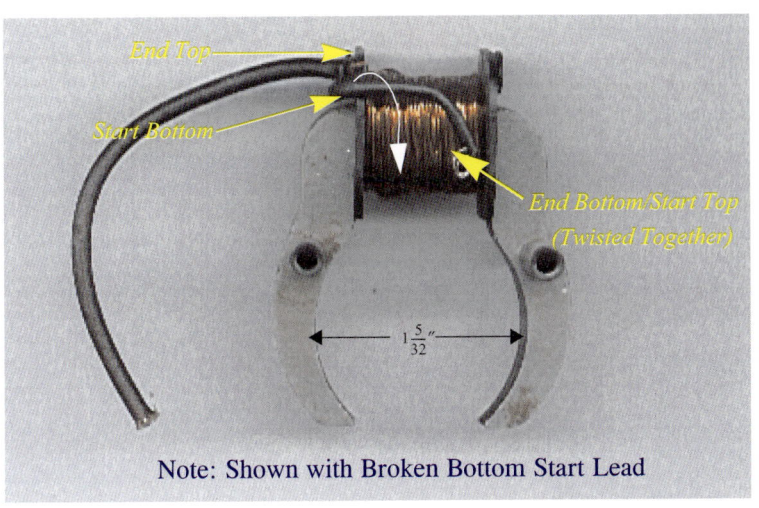 #282R	*Wire Size:*	28 (0.0121)
	# of Turns:	Top: 176 - 185 Bottom: 169 - 196
	Style:	Layered ...
	# of Layers:	4 (ea. coil)
	Resistance :	Top: 2.4 - 2.7 Ω Bottom: 2.2 - 2.3 Ω
	Thickness:	15/32"

Double-Wound (2 Stacked Layers) Field

The #282 Clutch Solenoid Coil (282-20)

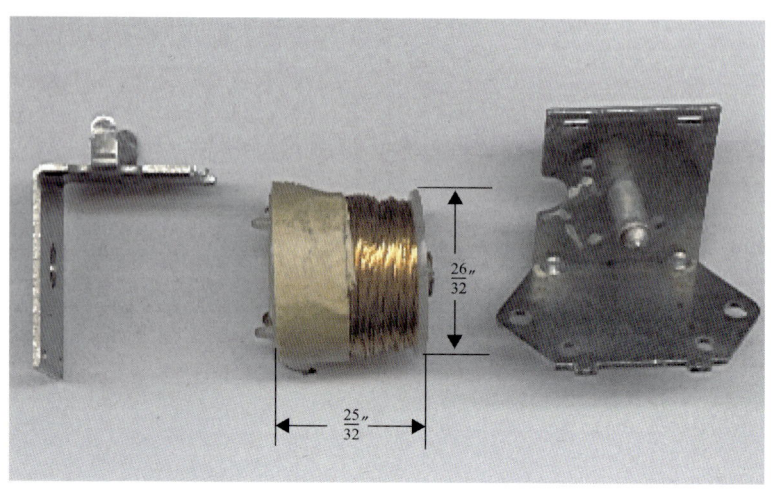

Part Detail	Specifications	
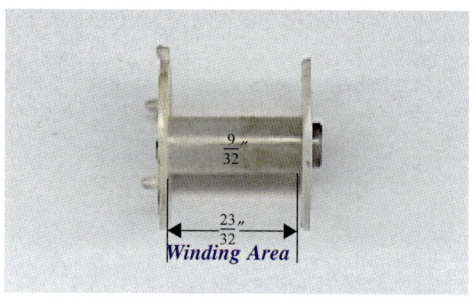	Wire Size:	29 (0.0110)
	# of Turns:	1285
	Style:	Layered ... but
	# of Layers:	@22
	Resistance :	14.9 - 15.0 Ω

The #282R Clutch Solenoid (282-156)

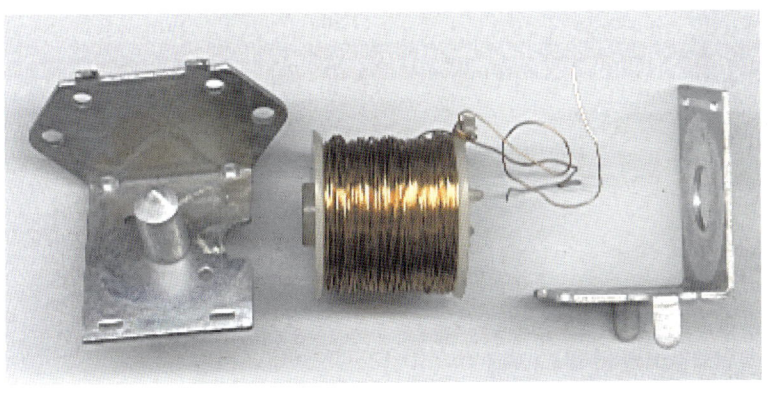

Part Detail	Specifications	
	Wire Size:	29 (0.0110)
	# of Turns:	1028
	Style:	Layered
	# of Layers:	18
	Resistance :	12.8 - 12.9 Ω

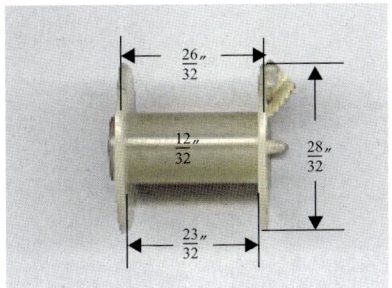

The #282/#282R Electromagnet (282-65)

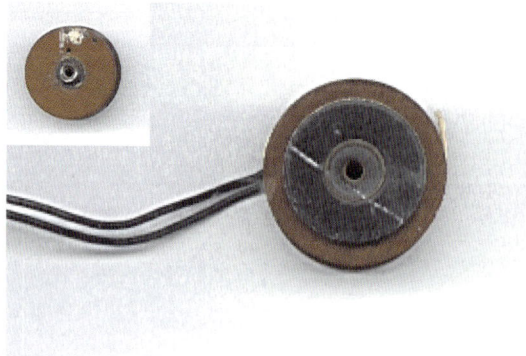

(Note: From a 282)

Part Detail	Specifications	
	Wire Size:	32 (0.0076)
	# of Turns:	911
	Style:	Random
	# of Layers:	Indeterminate
	Resistance :	22.0 - 22.1 Ω

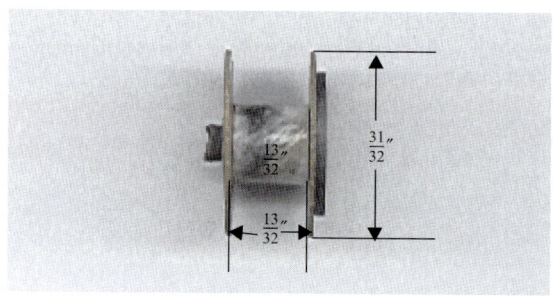

✱ *The #299 Code Transmitter Set* ✱

The 299 Code Transmitter Buzzer Coil (299-19)

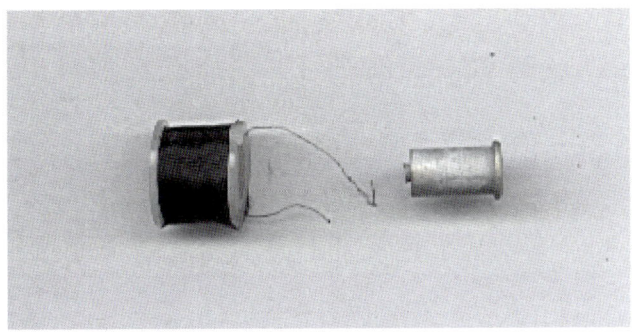

Part Detail	Specifications	
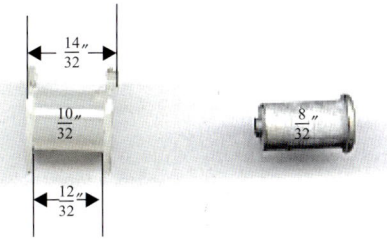	*Wire Size:*	35 (0.0053)
	# of Turns:	863
	Style:	Random
	# of Layers:	Indeterminate
	Resistance :	30.0 - 30.1 Ω

(Note: Red dots show coil soldering points).

✳ The #313 Bascule Bridge Motor ✳

The #313 Bascule Bridge Armature (313M-10)

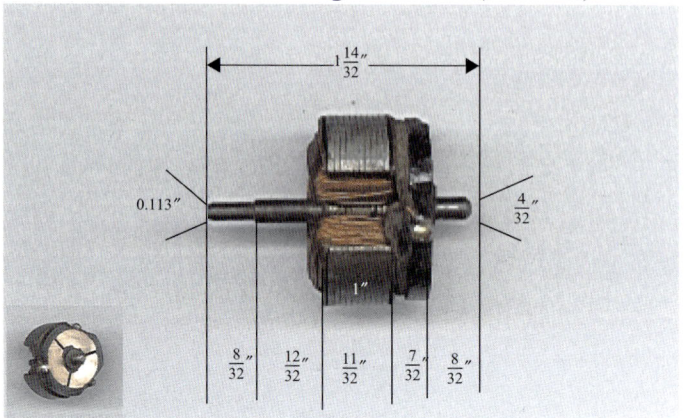

Motor Detail	Specifications	
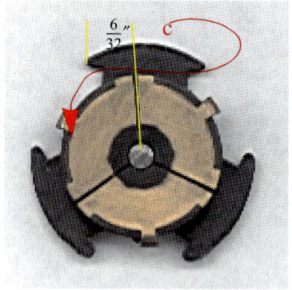	Wire Size:	27 (0.0135)
	# of Turns:	60
	Style:	Layered
	# of Layers:	6
	Direction:	Clockwise
	Resistance:	1.2 Ω
	Tie-Off:	Common

The #313 Bascule Bridge Field

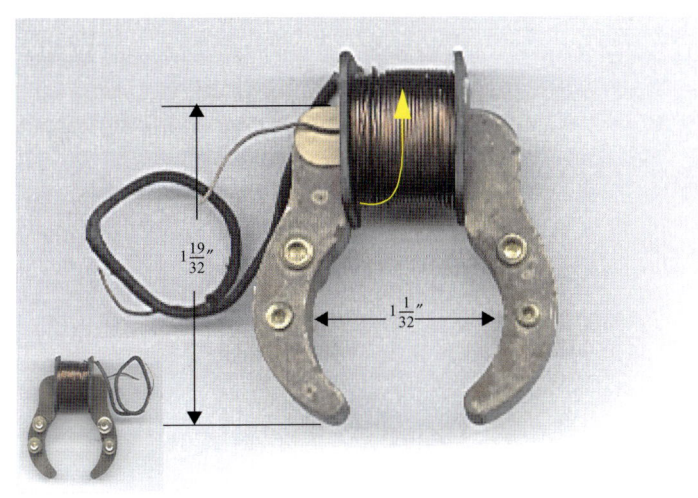

Motor Detail	Specifications	
	Wire Size:	24 (0.0190)
	# of Turns:	183
	Style:	Layered
	# of Layers:	8
	Resistance :	1.1 Ω
	Thickness:	11/32"

✳ The #334 Operating Dispatch Board ✳

The 334 Dispatch Board Motor (334-40)

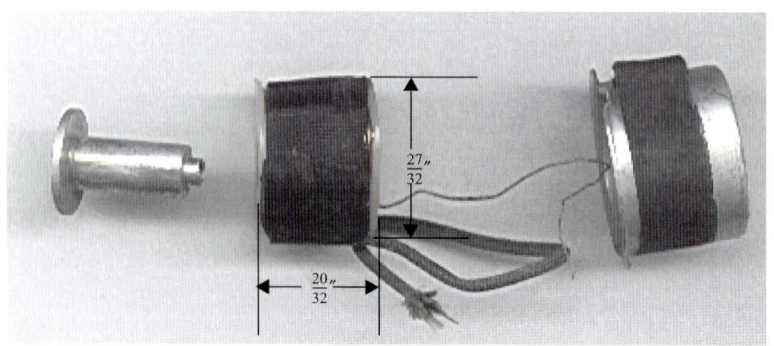

Part Detail	Specifications	
	Wire Size:	29 (0.0110)
	# of Turns:	768
	Style:	Layered ...
	# of Layers:	@16
	Resistance :	9.1 - 9.2 Ω

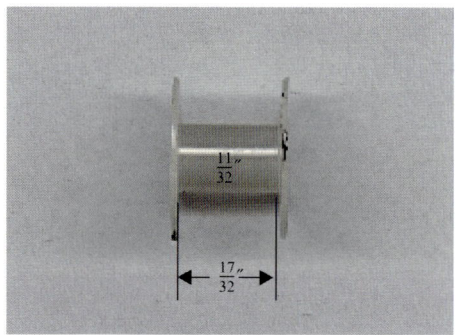

✳ The #342 Culvert Pipe Loader ✳

The 342 Culvert Pipe Loader (342-106)

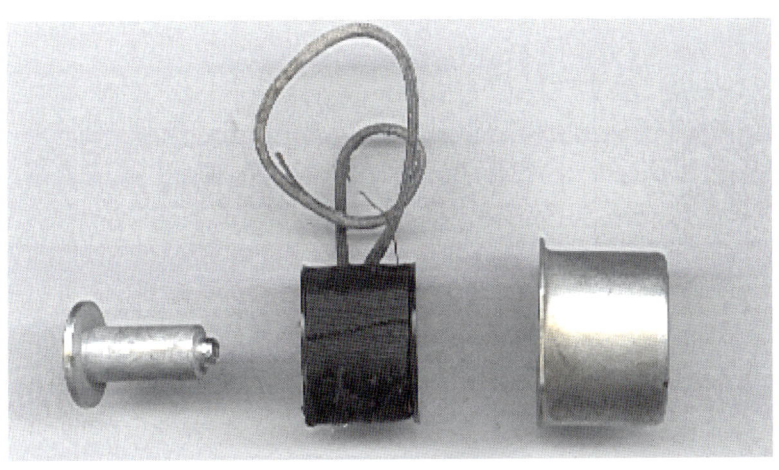

Part Detail	Specifications	
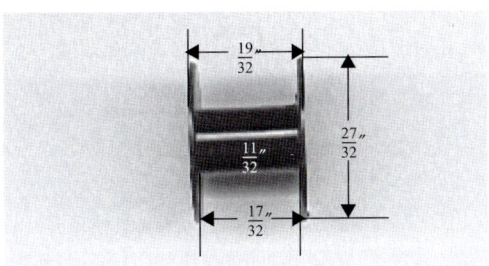	Wire Size:	29 (0.0108)
	# of Turns:	767
	Style:	Random
	# of Layers:	@18
	Resistance :	9.4 Ω

✳ *The #345 Culvert Pipe Unloader* ✳

The 345 Culvert Pipe Unloader (345-117)

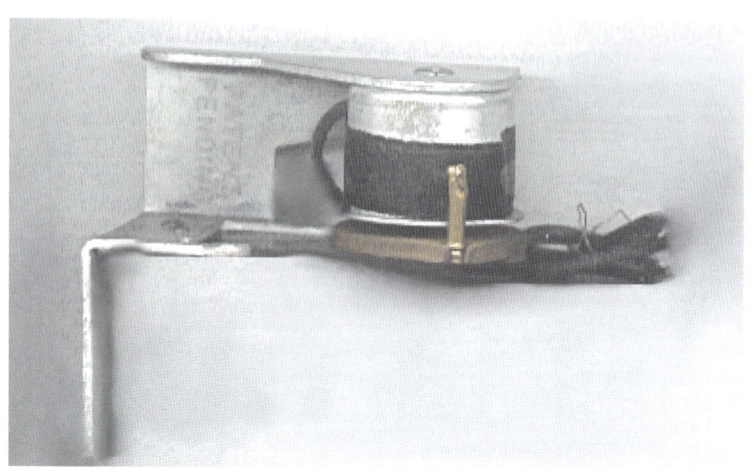

Part Detail	Specifications	
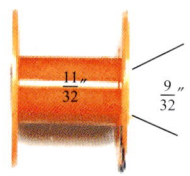	Wire Size:	29 (0.0108)
	# of Turns:	767
	Style:	Random
	# of Layers:	@18
	Resistance :	9.7 Ω

✸ *The #350 Transfer Table Motor* ✸
✸ *The #497 Coaling Station Motor* ✸

The motors used in the #350 and #497, are similar to the ones used in the #364 and #397 with the exception of the mounting brackets/method, and the fact that motors described here have a double (stacked) wound field.

#350 Transfer Table Motor

#497 Coaling Station Motor

The #350/#497 Armature (364M-5)

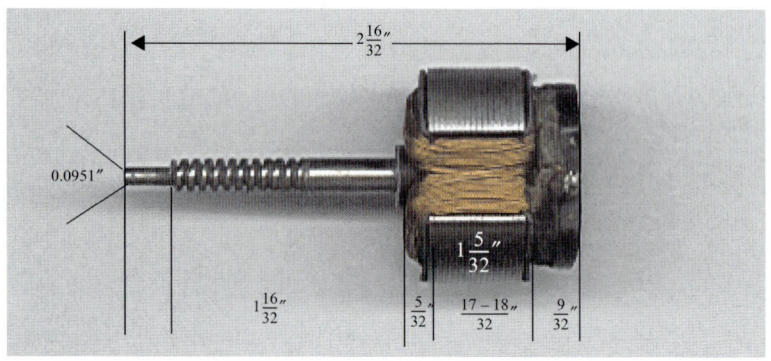

Motor Detail	Specifications	
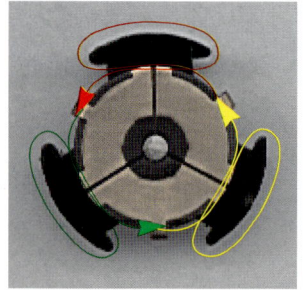 *The #350*	Wire Size:	28
	# of Turns:	130
	Style:	Layered
	# of Layers:	10
	Direction:	Clockwise
	Resistance :	1.3 - 1.4 Ω
	Tie-Off:	End-To-End

The #350/#497 Motor Field

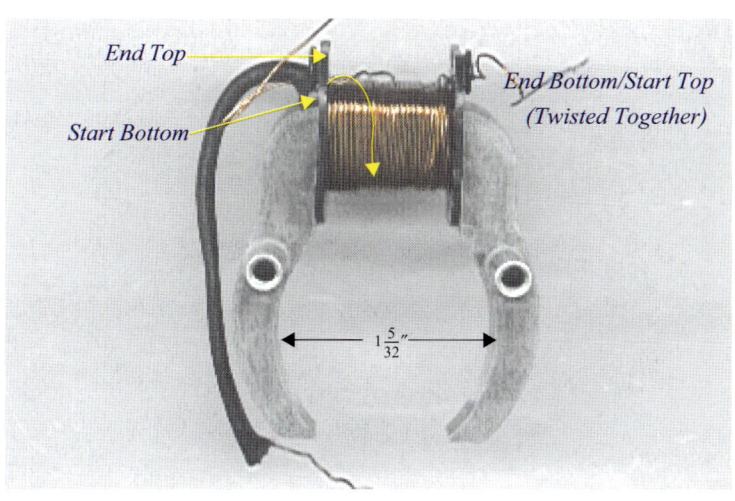

Motor Detail	Specifications	
	Wire Size:	26
	# of Turns:	107 (ea. layer)
	Style:	Layered
	# of Layers:	3 (ea. coil)
	Resistance :	Top: 1.1 Ω
		Bottom: 1.0 Ω
The #497	Thickness:	15/32" - 16/32"

Double-Wound (2 Layers) Field

The #497 Coaling Station Chute Coil & Bracket Assembly (497-44)

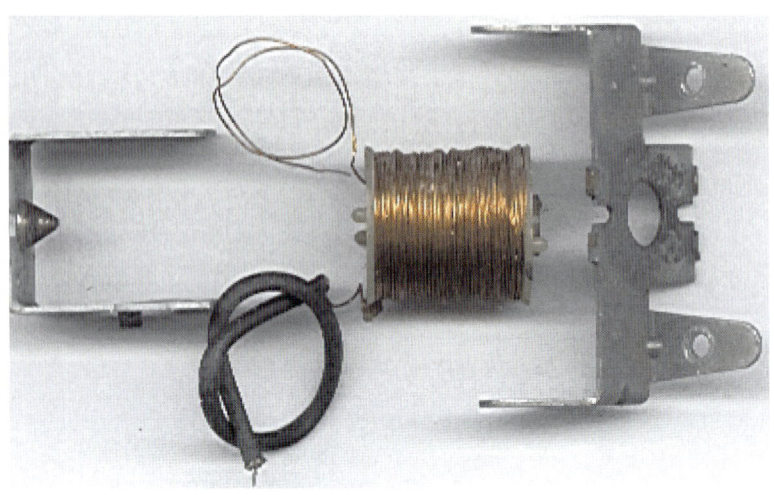

Part Detail	Specifications	
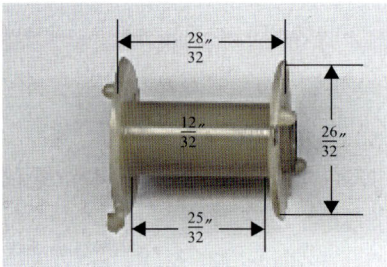	Wire Size:	27 (0.0135)
	# of Turns:	680
	Style:	Layered
	# of Layers:	14
	Resistance :	5.6 - 5.7 Ω

✳ The #352 Icing Station ✳

The 352 Icing Station Coil (352-33)

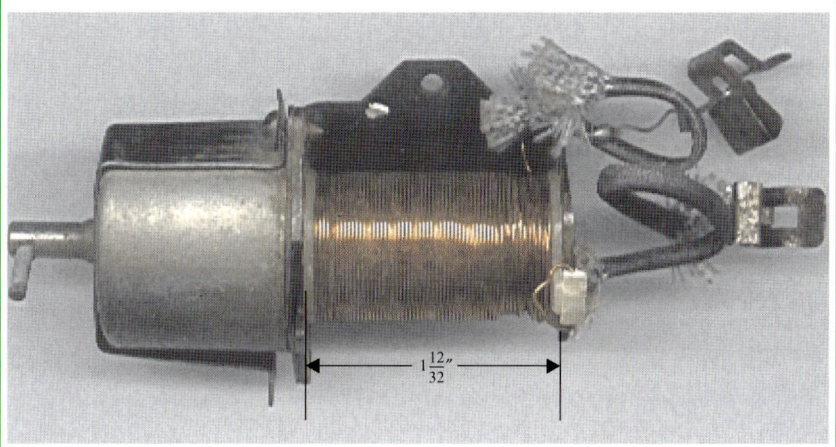

Note: Corroded Fahnstock Clips = High-Ω connection.

Part Detail	Specifications	
	Wire Size:	26 (0.0151)
	# of Turns:	550
	Style:	Layered
	# of Layers:	8
	Resistance :	2.1 - 2.2 Ω

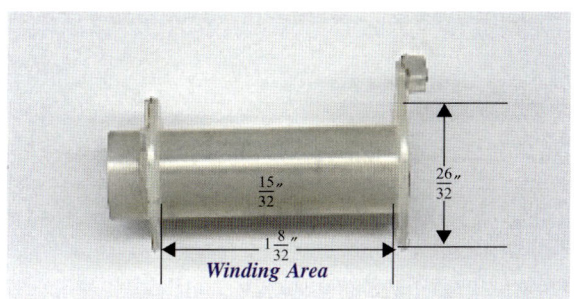

✸ *The #356 Operating Freight Station* ✸

The 356 Operating Freight Station Coil (356-50)

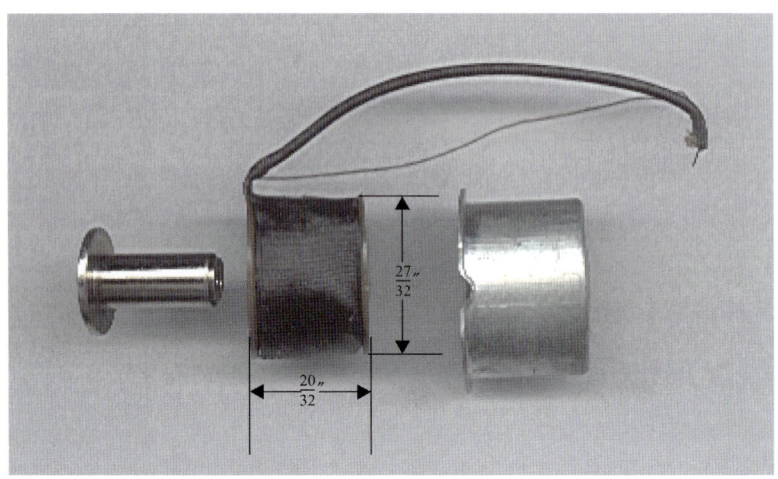

Part Detail	Specifications	
	Wire Size:	30 (0.0099)
	# of Turns:	926
	Style:	Random
	# of Layers:	Indeterminate
	Resistance:	13.5 - 13.7 Ω

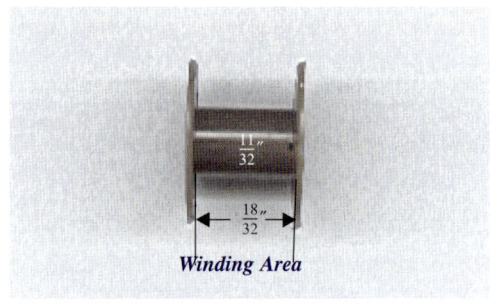

Winding Area

✷ *The #362 Barrel Loader* ✷

The 362 Barrel Loader Coil(362-20)

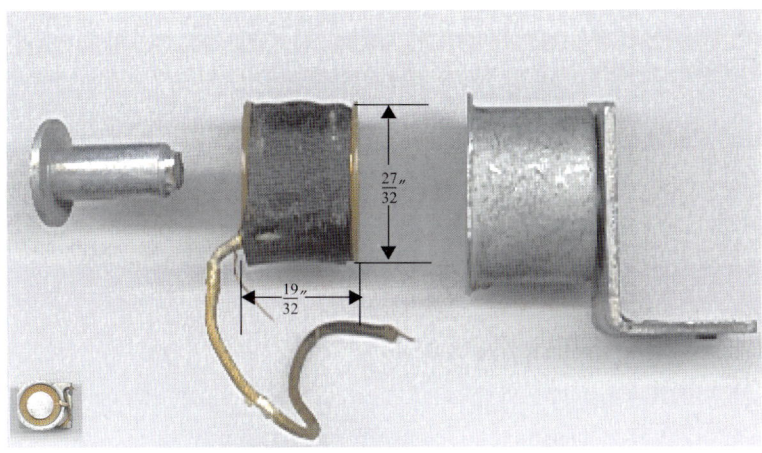

Part Detail	Specifications	
	Wire Size:	29 (0.0110)
	# of Turns:	792
	Style:	Random
	# of Layers:	@20
	Resistance :	9.4 - 9.5 Ω

(Note: Original bobbin was white nylon. This one overheated).

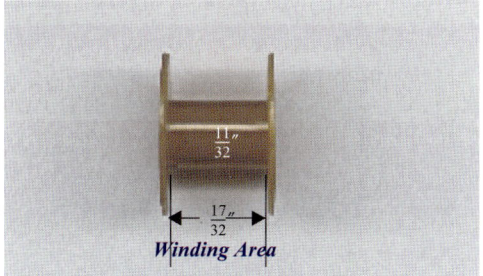

✲ *The #364 Lumber Loader Motor* ✲
✲ *The #397 Coal Loader Motor* ✲

The motors used in the #364 and #397, are similar to the ones used in the #350 and #497 with the exception of the mounting brackets/method, and the fact that motors described here use a single-wound field.

#364 Lumber Loader

#397 Coal Loader

The #364/#397 Armature (364M-5)

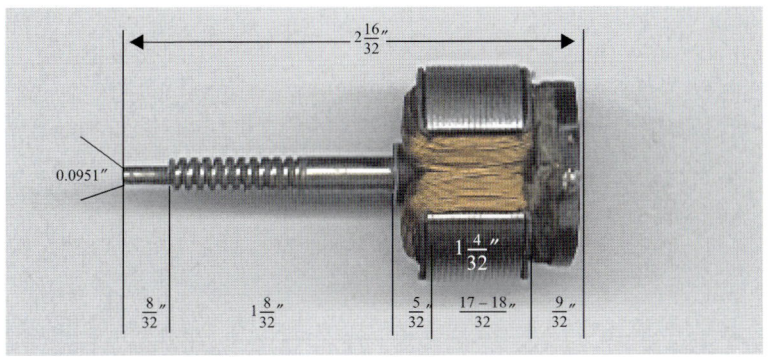

Note: Brown Insulators on #364; Black Insulators on all later armatures.

Motor Detail	Specifications	
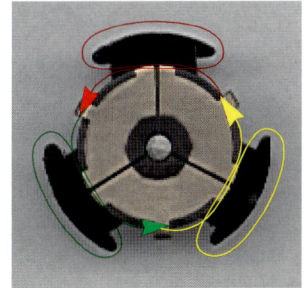 The #364	Wire Size:	28
	# of Turns:	130
	Style:	Layered
	# of Layers:	10
	Direction:	Clockwise
	Resistance:	1.3 - 1.4 Ω
	Tie-Off:	End-To-End

The #364/397 Motor Field

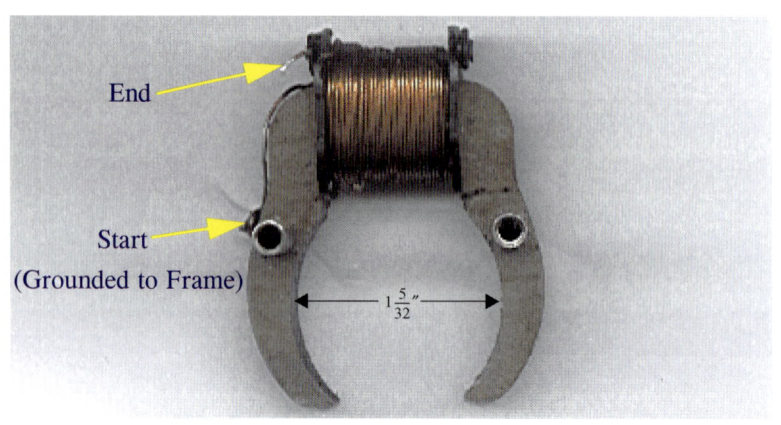

End
Start
(Grounded to Frame)
$1\frac{5}{32}"$

Motor Detail	Specifications	
	Wire Size:	23
	# of Turns:	150 - 156
	Style:	Layered
The #397	# of Layers:	6
	Resistance :	.9 - 1.0 Ω
	Thickness:	15/32" - 16/32"

✱ *The #375 Turntable* ✱

The 375 Turntable Motor (375-27)

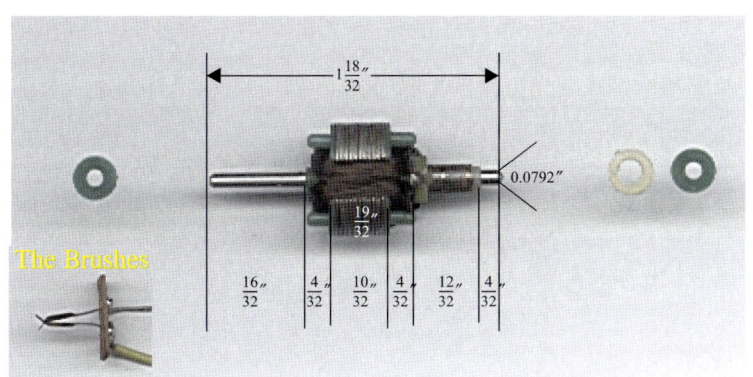

Part Detail	Specifications	
	Wire Size:	32 (0.0078)
	# of Turns:	150
	Style:	Random
	# of Layers:	Indeterminate
	Direction:	Counter-Clockwise
	Resistance :	1.9 - 2.0 Ω
	Tie-Off:	End-To-End

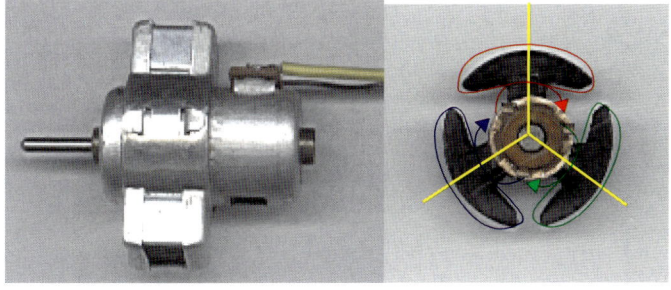

✻ *The #415 Fueling Station* ✻

The 415 Fueling Station Coil (415-40)

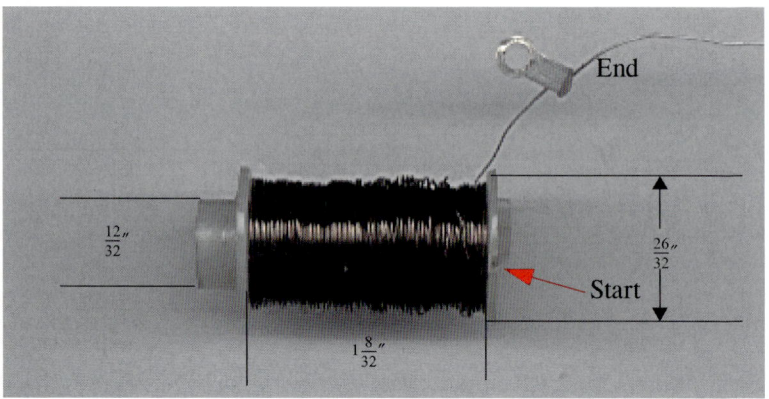

Part Detail	Specifications	
	Wire Size:	27 (0.0139)
	# of Turns:	555
	Style:	Layered
	# of Layers:	8
	Resistance :	4.4 - 4.5 Ω

Note: Another coil where the start lead tends to break off if put under pressure.

✴ *The #445 Switch Tower* ✴

The 445 Switch Tower Coil (445-10)

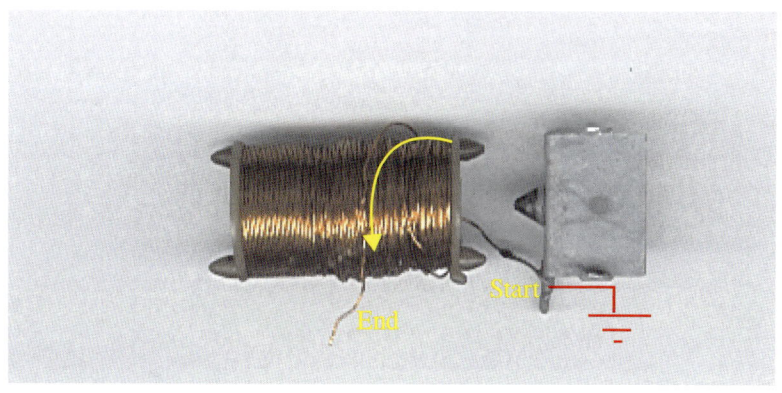

Part Detail	Specifications	
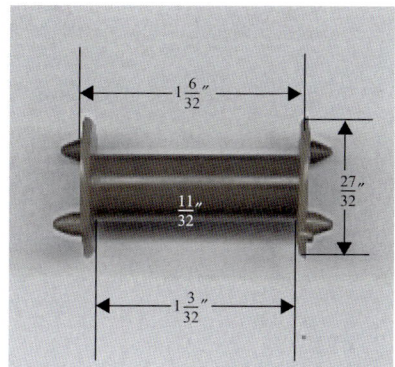	Wire Size:	27 (0.0135)
	# of Turns:	770
	Style:	Layered ...
	# of Layers:	@12
	Resistance :	5.7 - 5.8 Ω

O-Gauge - Lionel Postwar Reference Manual

✶ The #455 Operating Oil Derrick ✶

The 455 Operating Oil Derrick Solenoid (455-64)

Part Detail	Specifications	
	Wire Size:	28 (0.0123)
	# of Turns:	1014
	Style:	Layered
	# of Layers:	12
	Resistance :	9.1 - 9.2 Ω

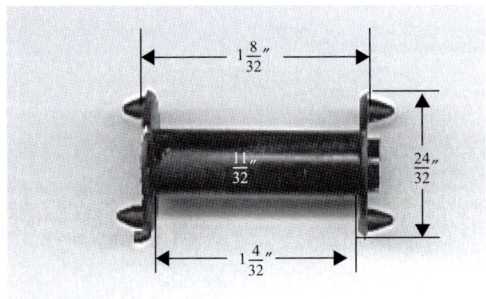

✲ The #456 Coal Ramp Set ✲

The 456 Coal Ramp Electromagnet (456-54)

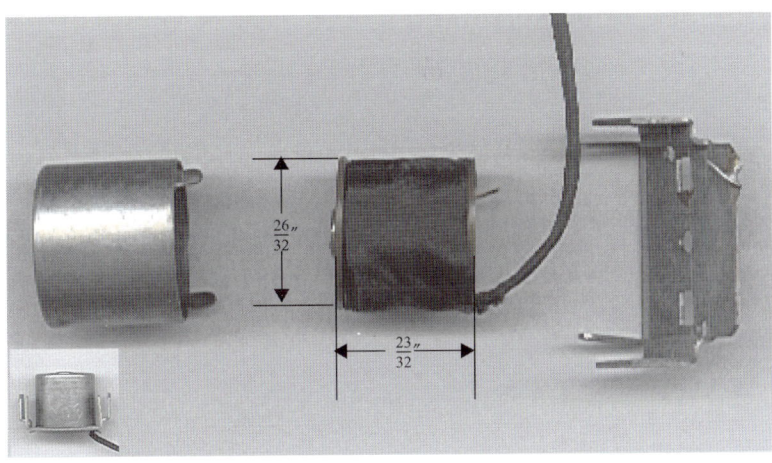

Part Detail	Specifications	
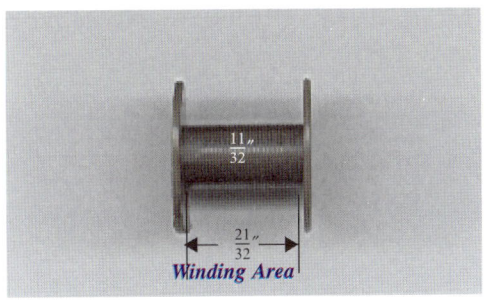	Wire Size:	26 (0.0155)
	# of Turns:	427
	Style:	Layered
	# of Layers:	12
	Resistance :	2.5 - 2.6 Ω

* *The #464 Operating Lumber Mill* *

The 464 Lumber Mill Vibrator Motor (464-45)

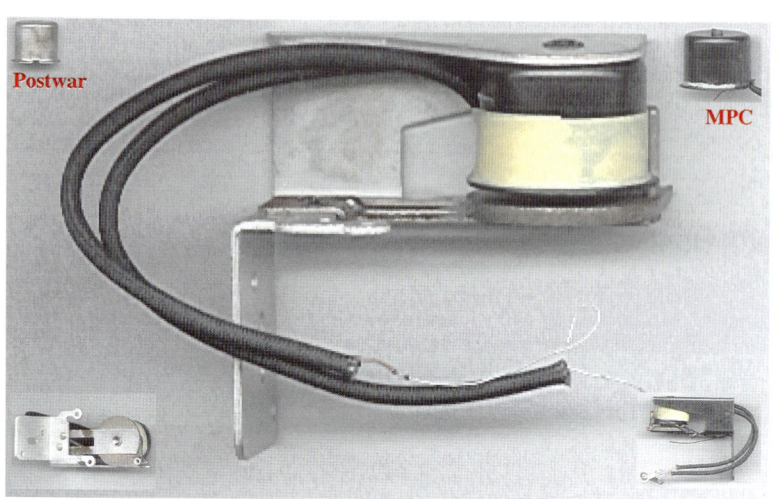

(Note: Postwar Casing Natural; MPC Casing Blackened).

Part Detail	Specifications	
	Wire Size:	29 (0.0110)
	# of Turns:	750
	Style:	Random
	# of Layers:	@18
	Resistance :	9.5 - 9.7 Ω

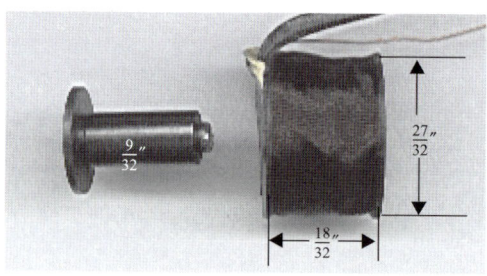

✶ *The #494 Rotary Beacon* ✶

The 494 Rotary Beacon Coil (494-40)

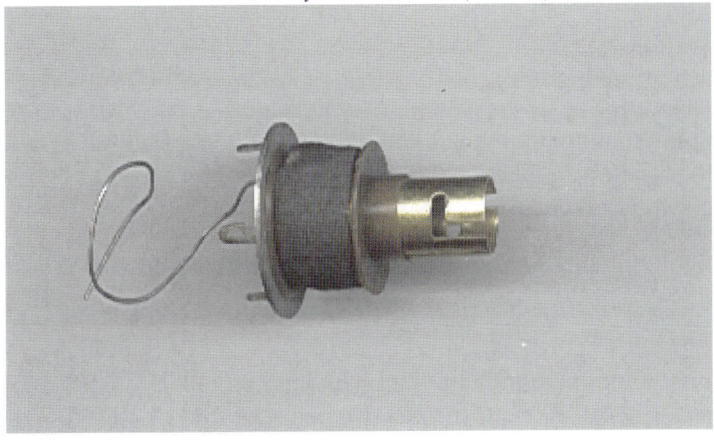

(Cf. #3520 Searchlight Coil)

Part Detail	Specifications	
	Wire Size:	31 (0.0084)
	# of Turns:	856
	Style:	Layered
	# of Layers:	20
	Resistance :	15.4 Ω

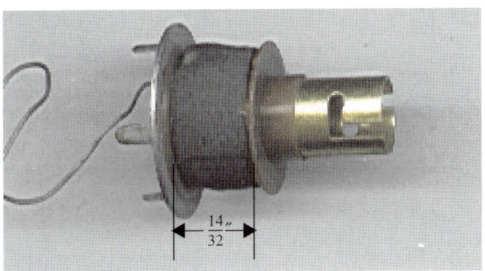

✻ *The #1045 Automatic Crossing Watchman* ✻
The #1045 Coil (1045-5)

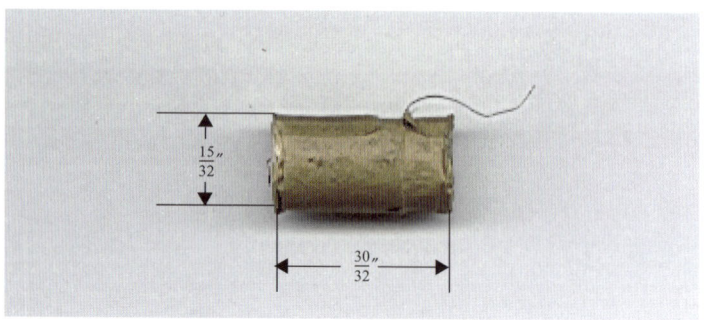

(Note: Coil & bracket assy 1045-13)

Part Detail	Specifications	
	Wire Size:	32 (0.0074)
	# of Turns:	1100
	Style:	Layered
	# of Layers:	12.75
	Resistance :	17.2 - 17.6 Ω

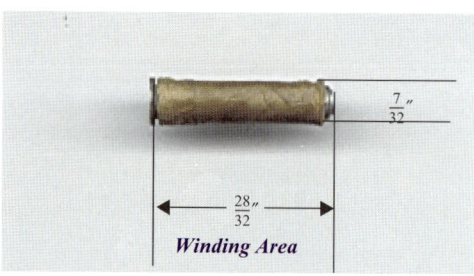

CHAPTER 6 *Remote Control Track & Switches*

This chapter provides an overview of the various remote control track mechanisms and switches used by Lionel during the postwar years. Many improvements were made to the basic remote control switches over the life of their production. As documented, these changes were limited to improved mechanical components (springs, gears, lamp-holders, etc.). So, it is entirely possible that other coil variations exist.

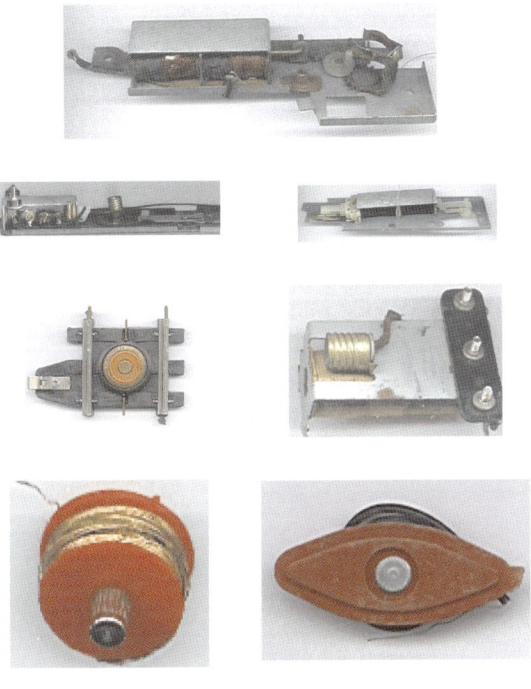

* *The #022 Remote Control Switch* *

The #022 Switch Coil (711-202)

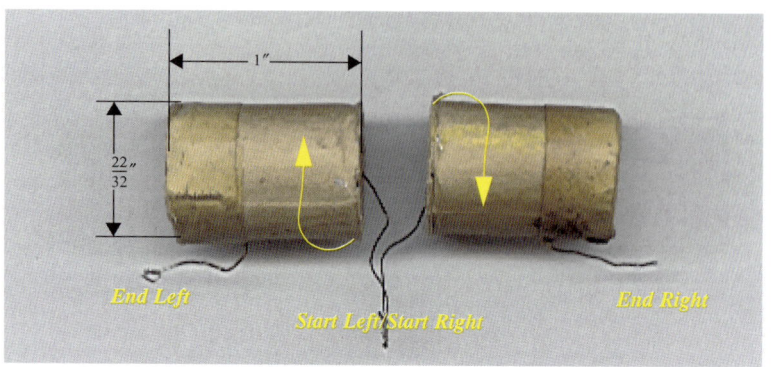

(Note: Each coil wound in same direction. Reversal occurs when mounted in motor).

Part Detail	Specifications	
1949 / *1950+*	Wire Size:	28 (0.0122)
	# of Turns:	641
	Style:	Layered
	# of Layers:	11
	Resistance :	5.7 - 6.0 Ω

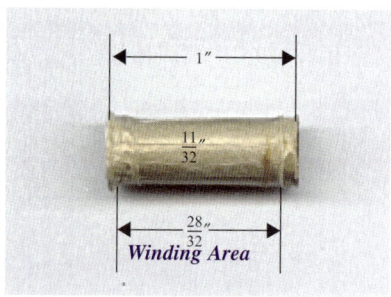

The #022 Switch Coil (711-127)

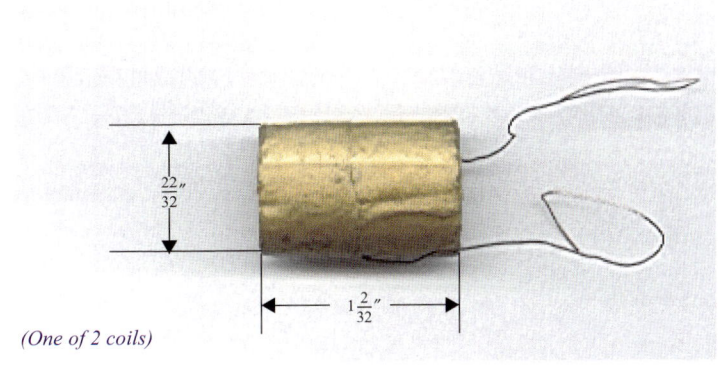

(One of 2 coils)

(Note: Same coil used in #151 Semaphore).

Part Detail	Specifications	
	Wire Size:	29 (0.0104)
	# of Turns:	720
	Style:	Layered
	# of Layers:	11.5
	Resistance :	8.0 - 8.2 Ω

✷ The #37 Uncoupling Section ✷

The #37 Uncoupling Section Coil (37-11)

Part Detail	Specifications	
	Wire Size:	30 (0.0098)
	# of Turns:	450
	Style:	Random
	# of Layers:	@17
	Resistance :	6.2 - 6.3 Ω

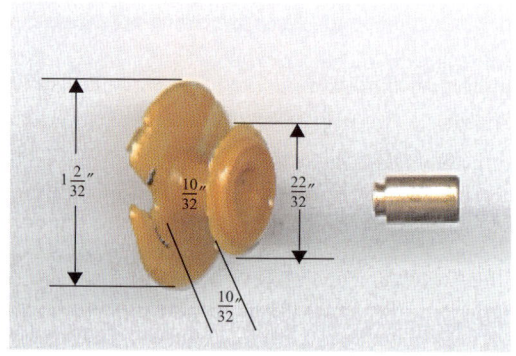

✳ *The #112 Remote Control Switch* ✳
✳ *The #112-1 Super O Switches* ✳
✳ *The #112R Super O Switches* ✳

The #112 RC Switch Motor (112-101/112-100)
The #112-1 Super O Switch Motors (112-229/112-230)

(Motors 112-229/112-230 were replacements for 112-101/112-100 Spring Change Only).

(Coil from 112-229/112-230 Shown Here)

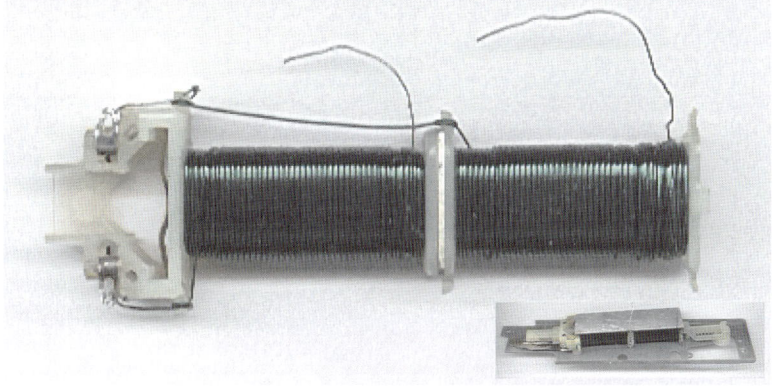

(Note: There Are Both Red- and Green-Enamelled Versions).

Part Detail	Specifications	
	Wire Size:	27 (0.0139)
	# of Turns:	550
	Style:	Layered
	# of Layers:	7
	Resistance :	3.7 - 3.8 Ω

(Rectangular Winding Arbor Measuring 8/32 High by 12/32 Deep).

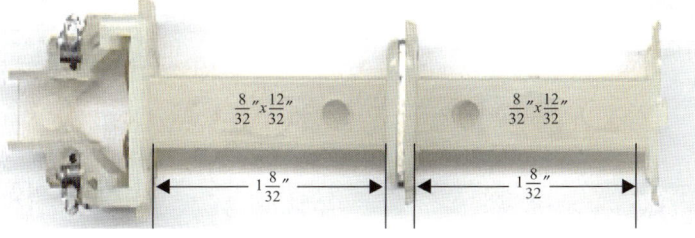

The #1121 O27 Switch

The #1121 027 Switch Motor Coil (1121-27)

Part Detail	Specifications	
	Wire Size:	29 (0.0107)
	# of Turns:	715
	Style:	Layered
	# of Layers:	11.5
	Resistance:	8.0 - 8.1 Ω

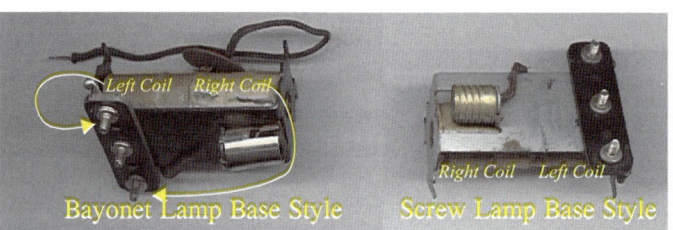

✳ The #1122 027 Remote Control Switch Coils ✳

The #1122 027 Switch Motor Coils

Part Detail	Specifications	
	Wire Size:	29 (0.0109)
	# of Turns:	862 (ea. coil)
	Style:	Random
	# of Layers:	@12-14
	Resistance :	9.0 - 9.1 Ω

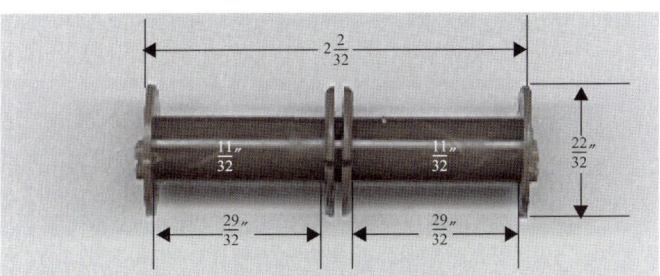

✻ The #6009 Remote Control Track Coil ✻
✻ The #6019 Remote Control Track Section Coil ✻
✻ The #6029 Remote Control Track Coil ✻

The #6009/#6019/#6029 Electromagnet Assembly (6019-31)

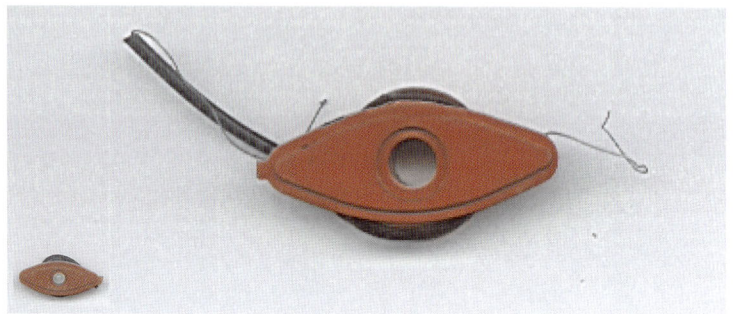

Part Detail	Specifications	
	Wire Size:	29 (0.0109)
	# of Turns:	450
	Style:	Random
	# of Layers:	@18
	Resistance :	5.0 - 5.1 Ω

The UCS Remote Control Track
The UCS Magnet Coil Assembly (UCS-11)

Part Detail	Specifications	
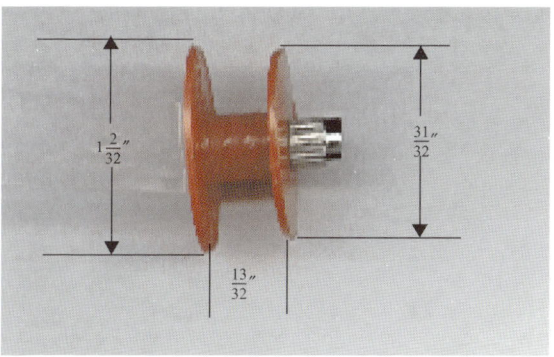	*Wire Size:*	27
	# of Turns:	530
	Style:	Layered
	# of Layers:	25
	Resistance :	4.8 Ω

CHAPTER 7 *Troubleshooting & Repair*

To date, troubleshooting of the coils in these units has necessarily been limited to "Good Coil"/"Bad Coil" decisions based on continuity alone. The bulk of the repair effort was then directed to mechanical adjustments, repairs and parts replacements. With the information in this manual, you can now make educated evaluations of both the electrical and the mechanical condition of the units.

 Volume I discussed the selection of a multimeter and how to take measurements. It also discussed recognition of commutator and bearing/bushing problems. The same concepts apply here.

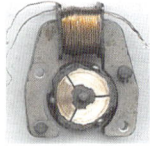 You might expect that a manual dedicated to documenting electrical characteristics would tout armatures, fields, and bobbins as the solution to all operational problems. That is not the case here. The fact is, these are electro-mechanical devices and their proper  operation requires that the electrical (wound) components work in concert with the mechanical components, and vice versa. So, focusing on one to the exclusion of the other could very well result in either a totally failed repair attempt, or a repair that results in minimum performance.

The sections which follow should be taken as an overview of the electro-mechanical dependencies inherent in the devices presented in this manual. An entire book could be (and probably will be) written on each of the broad classes of units described below.

✻ *Motorized Units* ✻

Most of the small "motorized units" in this volume face the same performance issues as their larger counterparts in Volume I. They are all subject to the cumulative effects of bearing and bushing wear.

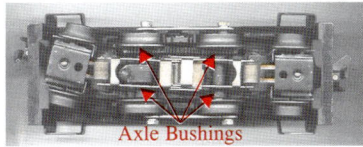

As built, most of these units were relatively small, and were designed for operation at low voltage. The gear ratio employed on some of the units guaranteed that they would creep (not fly) down the track. (E.g., see the operating description of the #60 Trolley in any of the *References*).

Today, many of these units can barely pull their own weight along the track. And quiet running? Well, it's been said that a blender chopping ice-cubes makes less noise than most of the switchers and trolleys that are still in service.

#50 Gang Car

The figures to the left and right show the armature bearing design typical of the small switchers, gang car, maintenance car and trolley. All the components rigidize the armature and prevent any play in the vertical or horizontal direction. The brush plate itself has no bushing, so maintaining a truly vertical position depends entirely on the lower thrust/guide bearings (red arrows in the figures) and the ball bearings (blue arrows).

#41 Switcher

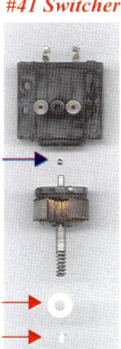

It is common to find brush plates where the ball-bearing has been drilled through the nipple between the brush tubes. These units cannot be operated without the ball bearing in place. It is also common to find units where the thrust/guide bearings have been cracked, broken, reamed out or hardened to the point that they no longer hold any lubrication. Noisy operation returns only 30 seconds or so after the motor is powered up. A comprehensive list of these "critical" parts is presented later in this chapter. In the meantime, the main causes of failure are discussed in the following sections.

Lack of Service

Lack of adequate servicing over the years has taken the greatest toll on these units. It is likely that most units have not had a complete cleaning since they left the factory. The biggest culprit is the "Internal Reservoir" documented in the service sheets for those units with a heavy cast frame. This is listed as being "filled at the factory and requiring no further attention."

The truth of the matter is that all of the units presented here require much more attention than the service sheets imply. The designers of these motors could not possibly have imagined the neglect to which these motors would be subjected and the amount of debris that would accumulate in the motor cavities (including ball-bearings, pieces of carbon brush material, sand, human hair, pet hair, rug fuzz, and spring fragments).

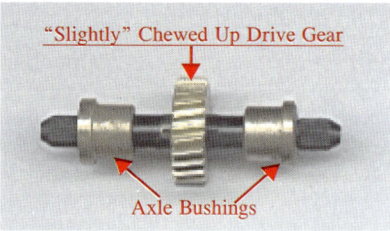

This floating debris eventually will find its way onto the drive gears and into the axle bushings. The effects of a ball-bearing or spring fragment flying around in the reservoir will be much more pronounced than the "slight" wear damage to the drive/worm gear shown in the foregoing figure.

So, if your unit hasn't had a major cleaning in recent memory, you might want to take a look "under the hood", and consider undertaking a major cleanup.

Over-Voltage Operation

Most of the motors in this section were designed to be operated between 9-14 volts. In fact, the motors appear to saturate at 10-11 Volts, and that's also the point at which they stop accelerating. Combine this with worn bearings and the natural inclination has always been to "increase the voltage" to the track (or swap in a higher voltage transformer) to get more speed out of the unit. Over the years, this "high voltage operation" has taken its toll on the windings, as described below.

Phase I

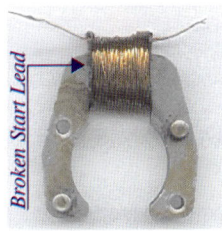

Years of high current/high temperature operation have made the windings extremely brittle. The act of removing the brush plate and bending it back to service the brushes or commutator incurs a major risk of breaking one or more leads. To avoid this risk, carefully unsolder all field leads before removing the brush plate or other contact plates configured on the unit.

Phase II

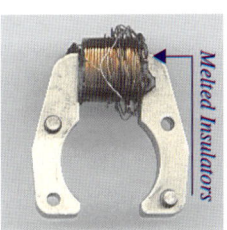

As the condition of the bearings/bushings progressively worsens, the motor develops more heat at any operating voltage. The heat (not operating power) is generated simply because the motor components are fighting to overcome mechanical deficiencies of the unit, and the armature simply cannot spin in phase with the voltage requirements. Meltdown of the insulators, quickly followed by shorting of the field windings is the natural fall-out of overheating.

If your unit is still in good operating condition, you can avoid future problems (like the ones described above), by simply backing off on the throttle (say about 10%-15%, or even more) once the unit has ceased accelerating. And, a yearly checkup/tune-up won't hurt either.

Performance-Critical Parts

The following parts should be considered critical to performance in most of the Motorized Units described in this manual. Any play or wear in these parts should be viewed with extreme suspicion. If there is any doubt, opting to replace or install them will only result in improved performance.

If the armature and field have been determined to be (still) "in-spec", a problem with these components will eventually lead to their failure. Sluggish, noisy and/or *very hot* operation of the unit are some of the symptoms attributable to these components when they begin to degrade. Left uncorrected, they could also attack and destroy the armature worm gear, rendering the armature useless. The good news is that many of the critical bearings and bushings referenced here are still available.

Consumables

Some parts were not meant to last *forever*. And if the parts inventory maintained by Lionel is any indication, many of the following parts were expected to be replaced periodically, if not every time a unit was serviced.

Cleaning burnt rollers, oil-impregnated brushes, and adjusting badly compressed or weakened springs can become a self-perpetuating activity if you attempt to push a part beyond its useful life. For example, compressed shoulder-brush springs will probably compress again when put back into service. They could even jam in the brush tubes after a period of operation, causing damage to the armature and field. As another example, oil impregnated carbon brushes will remain oil-impregnated, even if the surface oil is wiped off.

The following figure is intended to provide a list of generic parts which should be considered *consumable*. Part numbers are not provided, because individual units had their own unique part.

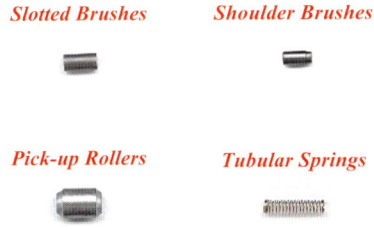

Given the relatively low price of the parts, cleaning them and putting them back into service could prove to be a major case of "false-economy". You may end up spending more time working on the units than enjoying them. Even worse, they could seriously damage a unit that is operated on a regular basis.

* *Whistles* *

Discussion of the mechanical factors affecting whistle performance is greatly simplified by the fact that there were only two *basic* types of whistles manufactured during the postwar years. These are shown in the following figure.

The WS-75 Diecast Motor

The WS-135/WS-181 Motor

Both of these whistles have two armature bearing points, as shown in the following figure. They consist of a rear bearing/bushing in the rear plate or motor frame, and an un-bushed hole in the brush plate.

WS-75 Bearing Points

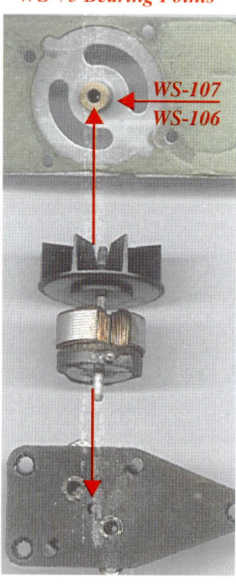

WS-135/WS-181 Bearing Points

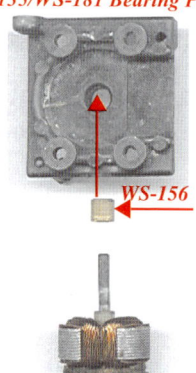

Enlargement of the bore at either of these bearing points can cause the following progressive stages of problems:

Initial — *Heavy vibration coming from whistle. Armature can't come smoothly up to speed when power is applied. Noticeably unacceptable delay before armature/impeller come up to speed and sound is generated.*

Intermediate — *When power is applied, a ratcheting/knocking sound is emitted from the whistle housing, accompanied by weak or intermittent tone generation.*

Terminal — *A loud "CLUNK!" is emitted from the whistle when power is applied. Armature locks in place. No sound is generated.*

An enlarged *brush plate* hole can be corrected in both whistles, by inserting a sleeve bearing into the hole. This always requires "reaming" of the hole and pressing the sleeve bearing into the brushplate. Most of the suppliers listed in Section 1 carry small brass or oilite bearings which are perfect for this application. Typical hand reamers are shown below.

Vise & Straight Reamer

Tapered Reamer

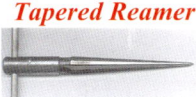

 The original WS-181/WS-135 *rear bearing plate* bearing is still available from some parts dealers. It is Part Number WS-156. The WS75 rear plate bearing (WS-107) and ball-bearing insert (WS-106) are more limited in availability, but can still be had from some parts dealers.

<u>Note</u>
Coagulated grease and warped frames are other conditions which can plague these whistles.

✻ *Accessories* ✻

As you have seen in this manual, Lionel used a whole range of devices to power its accessories. These devices can be broadly categorized as motors, magnets, and solenoids.

For motors, the "open-brush" motor was the type employed in the first half of the postwar years. The principles of trouble-shooting performance problems due to mechanical issues (gear, bushing and bearing wear) and their cumulative effects were covered in Volume I. The same principles apply here. In some cases, you may find yourself installing a brush-plate bearing where there was none before, as shown in the following figure.

The other motors, magnets and solenoids used in the accessories contained in this manual, also follow the same basic troubleshooting principles described in Volume I when it comes to taking readings. But they also have some unique peculiarities of their own.

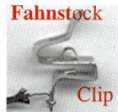  In general, measurements should be taken at the point at which power is applied: at the Fahnstock Clips or Binding Posts. Both should be examined for corrosion which could lead to a high resistance connection.

The "*motors*" described in the following sections present a kind of Catch-22. They depend on friction at their bearing points for proper operation. These friction/bearing points (at the hub of the wheels and pulleys, and strings wrapped around the pulleys) must never be lubricated. But unlubricated friction/bearing points must eventually wear out. In most cases, the only way to prevent their failure is reasonable periods of operation and keeping the mechanisms free of dirt, dust or other abrasives. The good news is, the coils in these "motors" do not depend on bushing condition for their survival.

✳ The "Vibrotor" Motor ✳

Lionel used two types of vibrating motors. The motor on the left (referred to as a "vibrotor" in the service sheets) consisted of a drive coil wound over a lamp socket. The "motor" required a drive washer and was used to rotate searchlight mechanisms. As you have seen in this manual, all of these "vibrotors" were wound identically.

The basic motor on the right was used in many different applications. It consisted of a coil which was housed in a "bell-shaped" housing or dome. In general, the core of the coil was a large rivet, which was also used to secure the assembly to a base or mounting bracket. Later versions of the housings were blackened. As you have seen in this manual, this "motor" was wound differently for different applications, even though the housings themselves would lead one to believe otherwise.

Proper operation of both of the motors in their basic form depends heavily on the condition of the "drive washer" (3520-16). The original "drive washer" was a simple rubber ring with three projections/fingers evenly spaced around its circumference. With time (and heat and motion) the projections tend to lay down flat or get worn off, and operation of the mechanism is impeded.

Later revisions of this "motor" specified use of a drive washer with six projections and a double-sided adhesive washer (3520-42). Note that the term "double-sided adhesive washer" is a bit misleading. The beige paper you see in the figure to the right on the 3520-42, encloses a circular dollop of adhesive. The paper itself is discarded once the drive washer is "glued" to the rotating element.

These parts are still available from most of the parts suppliers listed in this manual. See Greenberg's Repair and Operating Manual in the sections for the #3520/#3620 and the #3535. The same principles of operation apply to the #3530 Generator Car.

Note: A miniature version of this mechanism is contained in the #140 Banjo Crossing Signal which uses the 140-37 Adhesive Washer and the 140-32 Driving Washer.

✻ *The "String & Spring" Motor* ✻

The principle of the vibrating motor was also applied to driving the internal components of some of the larger accessories manufactured during this period. This application has been called (by) many names over the years, among them: The Snub & Slip Motor, The Grip & Slip Motor; the String & Spring Motor, etc., etc., etc. The basic motor is shown below.

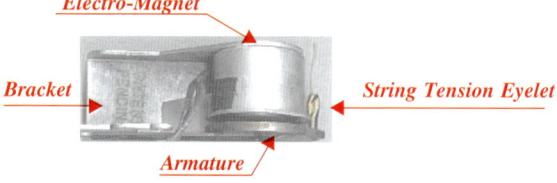

As you have seen throughout this manual, there was a degree of uniformity in the coils used in this motor. Once the variances in the turn-counts and minute differences in the resistance readings are digested, it can safely be stated that the same coil was used. The major differences in these motors was in the bracket, and in the positioning of the string tensioning eyelet.

From a #264

A good description of the operation and adjustment of these motors is contained in the Greenberg Repair and Operating Manual; especially in the sections describing the #464 Operating Lumber Mill and the #264 Fork Lift Platform.

After reading these descriptions (and in the absence of visible wear or damage to the spring, string, or gears on these units), you should be ready to agree that identifying or eliminating the "motor" coil and its electrical circuit as the cause of the problem is definitely the way to start troubleshooting these units.

In truth, the major cause of *electrical failure* of these units is accidental snapping off of a lead from a coil during maintenance. Loss of grip at the hub of the pulley wheel, stretching of the spring, and wear on the string are the main causes of *mechanical failure*. But over the years, other forces have been at work to degrade the operation, not only of these "motors", but of other accessories in this manual.

Soldering Joints

Degradation of forty-year old soldering joints is a major problem with these units. This is especially true of those units whose leads were "tack-soldered" to soldering lugs or to the coil frames. Tack soldering is a soldering technique that uses solder to create an electrical connection without first providing a clean, firmly wrapped mechanical connection at the soldering point. In many cases, the heat from the soldering iron was trusted to vaporize the enamel insulation on the wire.

This resulted in a high-resistance joint (sometimes three times higher than the documented resistance of the coil) which, as it aged, eventually prevented most of the available power from reaching the operating coil. In some cases, simply refreshing the soldering joint is adequate to correct the high-resistance connection. In other cases, a thorough cleaning (stripping) of the leads and soldering surfaces before resoldering will be required.

Coil Degradation

Many of the "String & Spring" coils in this manual were taken from "junker" bases. There was nothing mechanically wrong with the units, and the motors still vibrated when power was applied. The only problem was, the gear-train did not advance properly.   In approximately 38% of the cases, the problem was eventually traced to the coil.

Basically, the coil was found to be out-of-spec, sometimes due to shorted turns inside the coil (lower than expected reading), at other times, due to over-heated, brittle wire which had developed an abnormally high resistance (higher than expected reading). The one revelation that came from this exercise was that these coils don't just up and die, they degrade. If you're lucky, evidence of this degradation will take the form of over-heating.

The point of this discussion is that initially, when these accessories fail to operate satisfactorily, the probability that the problem is *electrical,* is *almost* equal to the probability that the problem is *mechanical*. Use the "*Resistance*" entry in the tables in this manual to quickly eliminate or identify the coil (or the electrical path) as a possible cause of problem.

✼ *Repairability Issues* ✼

If you look at the collage of mechanisms in the following figure, you will see a lot of rivet work (R), peened-over tube ends (P), and other heavy steel supports (S). Some pieces (as shown in the #264-101 figure below) are even spot-welded (W) in place. These all stand in the way of easy removal, repair and replacement of a burned out, or broken, coil.

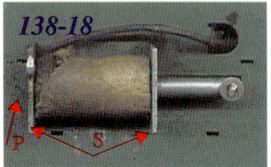
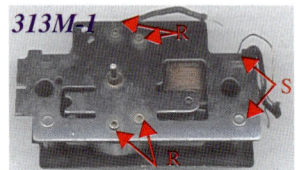

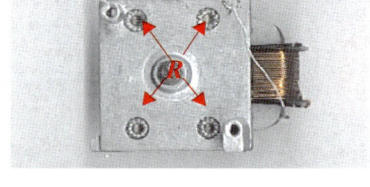

Post-1948 Whistle Motor Frame

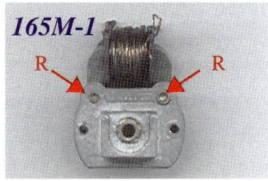
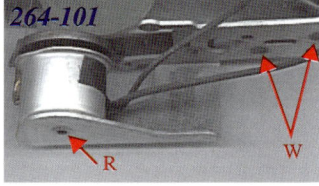

By definition, this is what is meant when a mechanism is described as "not meant to be repaired". And that, in fact, is the absolute truth. Many of the pieces in this manual were never meant to be repaired once they left the factory. They were meant to be replaced.

The fact that many of these assemblies (and subassemblies) are no longer available from the factory puts it squarely on the hobbyist's shoulders to undertake the repair when something catastrophic happens to these coils. It is simply not economically feasible to conduct this type of repair in a business environment, since the labor involved could well exceed the monetary or sentimental value of a unit by several times.

While detailed repair procedures are beyond the scope of this reference manual, sufficient queries were received after Volume I was published to justify a summary of the tools and supplies which can be brought to bear on the problem. An overview of these tools is provided in the paragraphs which follow. More detailed procedures will be published in future Maintenance & Repair manuals.

When conducting any of these repairs, it is important NOT to bend, twist, or remove any other parts; especially welds and other bracket mounting rivets. This will only compound any alignment/adjustment problems you will face when the unit is reassembled. For parallel-plate steamer motors, the side frame studs may also have to be drilled & tapped, but that's all.

Rivet tips can be removed by grinding or drilling. A Dremel tool equipped with a cutoff wheel is a good candidate for grinding.

Alternatively, the tips can be drilled off using an over-sized metal drill bit (a drill bit equal to or slightly larger than the diameter of the rivet tip).

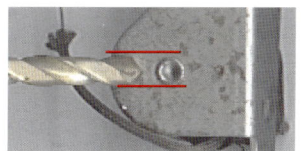

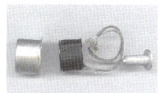

Regardless of the tool chosen, the rivet tip should be ground or drilled until flush with the frame. Do not drill all the way through the frame. The coil can then be pried or pressed from the bracket and disassembled.

Once the coil has been repaired, there are two choices to make. If a replacement rivet is available, reinstall the coil using the new rivet. In most cases, a directly substitutable rivet will not be available, and the old rivet will have to be drilled & tapped, and then "bolted" back onto the frame or bracket. Tapping is the process of creating threads where, before, there were none (e.g., after drilling a hole in metal).

So, the next step is to select a drill, tap and screw size that meets all of the following criteria. The shorter the length of the screw, the better. This will save a lot of time later, when it comes time to tap the hole.

The selected drill size must fit within the rivet tip, leaving the outer edge of the tip intact once the drilling is completed.

The screw required for the selected drill and tap must have a head slightly larger than the outer diameter of the rivet tip. The screw head must grip the frame when the coil assembly is bolted back in.

The following table provides the pairings of drill and tap/screw sizes you will find most useful in train and other household repairs. Numbered metal (*not* woodworking) drill bits and taps are available at some hardware stores and hobby shops. They are sometimes sold in packs containing a tap and its associated numbered (*not* fractional) drill bit. Large retailers also carry "Tap & Die" sets, which include a wider range of taps than needed here.

Numbered Drill	Tap/Screw Size
#51	2-56
#43	4-40
#36	6-32
#29	8-32

This may seem like a large number of drills, taps and screws to keep on hand. For reference purposes, 95% of all fields studs can be secured using the #51/2-56 combination. All steamer side frames can be secured using the #43/4-40 combination.

Finally, there are two tools that can be used to hold the tap. One is a "chucking" vise (shown on the right) and the other is a "pin vise". The advantage of a pin vise is that, if the tap jams during the tapping operation, the tap will begin slipping within the body of the vise, and will not break off inside the piece being tapped. The following figure shows a good quality pin-vise used for small taps (2-56 and smaller).

Once the hole is drilled in the material, the hole must be tapped to a depth slightly longer than the length of the threaded part of the screw. Twist the pin-vise/tap back and forth in the hole at most 1/4 turn at a time. Do not proceed deeper until the tap turns freely. Periodically stop, back the tap out, and dump any chips which may have been caught in the hole.

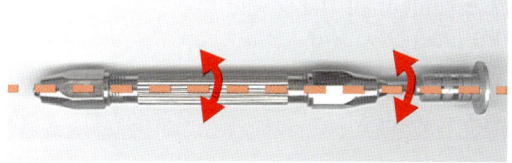

As shown in the figure above, the pin-vise, tap, and the piece being tapped must be kept aligned at all times. This will, for the most part, avoid bending the tap and snapping it off inside the hole.

So you see, these components can be repaired. The only limiting factor is the amount of time you are willing to spend on them. And most of the "unrepairable" units in this manual definitely *are!* worth the time.

Note:
An alternative to drilling and tapping is epoxying.
But the longevity of the fix using an epoxy is not predictable.

CHAPTER 8 *Conclusion*

✻ *Summary* ✻

Many of the electrical components in this manual (and its predecessor volume) ceased being available some 30 to 40 years ago. But many others continued to be produced through the end of the 20th Century (either as repair parts, or to support current production). The technology was changing, but the basic designs were solid and proven, and so continued in production. The components also underwent recognizable changes as the years progressed, in step with the latest technology, or as a result of design improvements. So, some components are backward compatible with their Postwar "Parents", some are not. The same is true if you are looking for parts that are "upwardly" compatible.

A good example of this can be found in the 2028-109 armature, whose evolution is shown below. The most obvious progression is in the commutator changes starting in 1963. But also notable were the gear changes, the replacement of the lower fiber sleeve with a Zytel sleeve, and finally with a steel clip. Not so noticeable is the switch from fiber coil insulators, to molded insulators, to high temperature epoxy resin insulation in the 1990s.

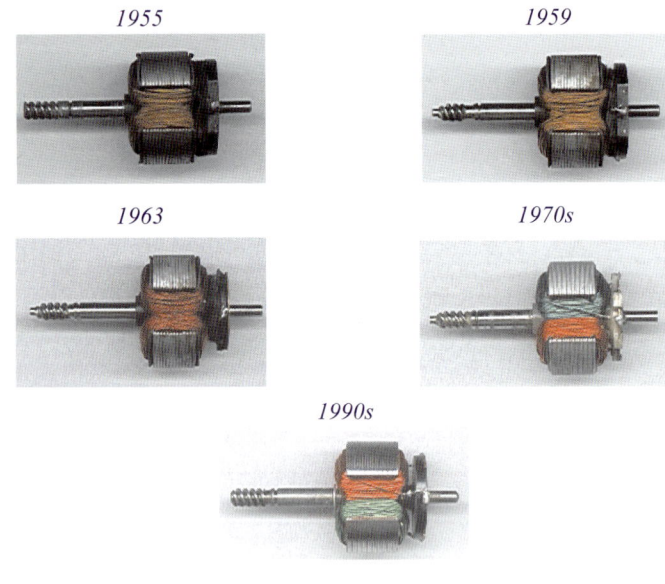

1955 *1959*

1963 *1970s*

1990s

Other units were also reproduced during the next three decades. Two of the more "stunning" examples are shown below. Some were near perfect copies of their predecessors, others incorporated major improvements in bearings and wire selection (all leading to cooler operation and, potentially, longer life).

The Ballast Tamper

#54 Ballast Tamper   #8578 Ballast Tamper

The Inspection Car

#68 Executive Inspection Car   #18447 Inspection Vehicle

So, yes ... there is a "sequel" to the Postwar years, in what has recently been labelled "The Modern Era" (1970 to present day). But that's another story altogether.

✸ *Support* ✸

The manual you have purchased comes with e-mail support, direct to the author. It also comes with web-based updates, which are free to all Registered Owners of this manual. Each manual is "Registered" to an individual person or shop.

If you have registered your copy and have an e-mail address, you will get a message notifying you when some new information is available on the web. You can then download and print the new information at your convenience. Your "Registration Number" is at the bottom of this page. So, don't delay. Register your copy today on the Internet at:

http://www.trainrefs.com

✳ ✳ ✳

200197